◆ THE FLAVORS OF ◆
BON APPÉTIT

◆ THE FLAVORS OF ◆

BON APPÉTIT

◆ 1999 ◆

from the Editors of Bon Appétit

Condé Nast Books ◆ Pantheon
New York

For *Bon Appétit* Magazine

William Garry, *Editor-in-Chief*
Laurie Glenn Buckle, *Editor, Bon Appétit Books*
Marcy MacDonald, *Editorial Business Manager*
Carri Marks, *Editorial Production Director*
Sybil Shimazu Neubauer, *Editorial Administrator*
Jordana Ruhland, *Assistant Editor*
Marcia Lewis, *Editorial Support*
Norman Kolpas, *Text*
H. Abigail Bok, *Copy Editor*
Gaylen Ducker Grody, *Research*
Jeanne Thiel Kelley, *Food Research*

For *Condé Nast* Books

Lisa Faith Phillips, *Vice President and General Manager*
Tom Downing, *Associate Direct Marketing Director*
Lucille Friedman, *Fulfillment Manager*
Colleen P. Shire, *Assistant Direct Marketing Manager*
Angela Lee, *Direct Marketing Associate*
Meredith L. Peters, *Direct Marketing Assistant*

Produced in association with Patrick Filley Associates, Inc.
Designed by Laura Hammond Hough

Front Jacket: Grilled Lobster Salad with Avocado and Papaya (page 105).

Back Jacket: Top: Honey Apple Pie (page 177);
Middle: Pan-fried Celery Root, Potato and Goat Cheese Terrine (page 114);
Lower Left: Poblano Potato Salad (page 158) and Super Slaw(page 150);
Lower Right: Cornish Game Hens with Orange and Honey (page 89).

Contents Page: Top: Spinach and Red Pepper Crostini (page 23);
Middle: Grilled Sea Bass, Mango, Grapefruit and Avocado Salad (page 92);
Bottom: Peach-Berry Upside-Down Crisp (page 184).

ISBN 0-375-40628-x

Manufactured in the United States of America

FIRST EDITION

2 4 6 8 9 7 5 3 1

Condé Nast Web Address: http://www.epicurious.com

Random House Web Address: http://www.randomhouse.com

◆ CONTENTS ◆

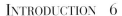

·INTRODUCTION·

Roast Chicken with Tarragon (page 76)

Trends. Almost every magazine worth its salt (or any other seasoning you might care to mention) watches them. That certainly holds true here at *Bon Appétit*, where, every day, we make every effort to keep track of the most significant trends in the way people cook, eat, dine out in restaurants and entertain at home.

We report on those trends in the magazine's regular columns such as Starters, Bon Vivant, People and Places, Going Out, The Restaurant Reporter and Diet Watch. We also reflect them in the recipes we feature in every issue. Sometimes, we modestly like to think, we even help to set the trends, building enthusiasm among our readers for newly popular preparations, foods, ingredients and cooking styles as diverse as smoothies, wild mushrooms, steaks, old-fashioned desserts, fusion cuisine and bistro cooking.

But, you might wonder, aren't only so many trends possible before history starts to repeat itself? Indeed, look up *trend* in a good dictionary and you'll discover that it comes to us from the Middle English word *trenden*, "to turn or revolve," which itself probably derives from the Middle High German *trendel*, "a disk or spinning top." In other words, trends can be circular: They keep going away and coming back, and what once was old is often new again.

Grilled Skirt Steak with
Cumin and Cilantro (page 49)

That certainly holds true for some of the trends you might discover when looking over the best recipes of the past year, collected here in *The Flavors of Bon Appétit*. Chief among them is a rediscovery of good old-fashioned home cooking. From Featherweight Buttermilk Biscuits (page 165) to Creamy Chicken-Noodle Casserole with Spinach and Mushrooms (page 80), Roast Chicken with Tarragon (page 76) to Bread and Butter Pudding (page 203), we're enjoying dishes again that remind us of the comforts of home.

Yet our growing knowledge of world cuisines continues to expand our definition of what might be labeled "home cooking." Few of us today think any longer of pasta or pizza, for example, as being strictly Italian, or consider various Latin American or Asian specialties to be foods you would only order off a restaurant menu. That is why such recipes as Onion and Poppy Seed Focaccia (page 165), Vietnamese-Style Spring Rolls with Shrimp (page 18) or Chicken and Green Olive Enchiladas (page 74) encourage us to prop open the book and start cooking—no special occasion required.

Truth is, we've all learned a lot more about food in recent years, and as a result we expect more of it. When we

Bread and Butter Pudding (page 203)

Linguine and Clams in
Ginger-Soy Broth (page 123)

Seafood Chowder with Dill (page 98)

prepare a recipe, good results just aren't good enough. We want flavors to be vivid and intense. That desire is reflected in recipe after recipe in this collection, many of which feature ingredients that turn up the flavor to full volume.

You'll find the sweet-hot taste of ginger, for example, lending its character to such dishes as Linguine and Clams in Ginger-Soy Broth (page 123), Pan-seared Tuna with Ginger, Miso and Cilantro Sauce (page 101) and Fresh Ginger and Citrus Sorbet (page 210). Pungent garlic punches up the flavor of recipes including Grilled Lamb Chops with Red Wine, Garlic and Honey Glaze (page 65) and Smoked Vegetables with Garlic Vinaigrette (page 147). Chili peppers contribute spicy heat to recipes such as Grilled Skirt Steak with Cumin and Cilantro (page 49), Poblano Potato Salad (page 158) and Cucumber, Radish and Green Onion Salad with Chili-Lime Dressing (page 150). And highly flavorful cheeses enrich such dishes as Goat Cheese Ravioli with Basil (page 22) and Grilled Burgers with Roquefort Mayonnaise and Barbecued Red Onions (page 51).

We're also cooking with more fresh herbs than ever before. Their presence is felt in every course of the meal, from such starters as Chilled Beet, Orange and Dill Soup (page 35) and Grilled Clams with Basil-Bacon Salsa (page 13); to main courses like Broiled Chicken with Thyme, Fennel and Peppers (page 84) and Seafood Chowder with Dill (page 98); to side dishes and salads, including Rosemary Mashed Potatoes (page 142) and Warm Green Bean Salad with Pine Nuts and Basil (page 154); to desserts even, such as Fruit Salad with Papaya-Mint Sauce (page 182).

We enjoy greater access to fresh herbs now, thanks to another phenomenon that exemplifies how new trends often mark the return of old-fashioned ways. A century ago, long before the advent of airfreight and deep-freezing, everyone cooked with the seasons and used locally grown or gathered produce. Today, in season, local vegetables and fruits are prized once more for their superior flavors, textures and nutrients. And they are available to us in ever-greater abundance thanks to enterprising food stores and produce shops and the proliferation of farmers' markets.

Fresh Blackberry Pie (page 172)

In page after page of this book, you'll find fresh evidence of this trend in recipes that, just a decade ago, might have required a home garden or a scavenger hunt for their featured ingredients. From Pan-fried Celery Root, Potato and Goat Cheese Terrine (page 114) to Mixed-Mushroom Lasagna with Parmesan Sauce (page 124), Fresh Blackberry Pie (page 172) to Asian Pears with Ginger Syrup (page 184), the way we cook and eat today revolves around a wondrous variety of readily available fresh produce.

Indeed, *variety* is a good word with which to sum up all the trends you will find in this latest collection of *The Flavors of Bon Appétit*. Home cooking; an international outlook; intense flavors; fresh fruits and vegetables that follow the seasons: Each, in its way, reflects the many options all of us now enjoy whenever we contemplate a meal. And, as the familiar (but usually misquoted) verse from eighteenth-century English poet William Cowper goes, "Variety's the very spice of life, That gives it all its flavour."

·STARTERS·

*Clockwise from top left: Spiced
Nuts (page 20); Spinach and
Red Pepper Crostini (page 23);
Orange-marinated Olives
(page 24); and Red Caviar Dip
with Asparagus, Fennel and
Radishes (page 22).*

A deliciously light alternative to chips and dip, this dipping sauce starts with nonfat yogurt and low-fat mayonnaise. Roasted peppers, chilies and green onions add interest. Begin making the sauce the day before serving since the yogurt needs to drain and thicken overnight.

♦ ♦ ♦

Artichokes with
Roasted Red Pepper Velvet

♦ ♦ ♦

¼ cup white wine vinegar
6 12- to 14-ounce fresh artichokes

Roasted Red Pepper Velvet (see recipe below)
½ teaspoon herbes de Provence*

Pour vinegar into small bowl. Cut stems and top 1½ inches off artichokes. Peel away tough bottom outer leaves from artichokes. Dip cut surfaces of artichokes into vinegar.

Cook artichokes in large pot of boiling salted water until knife pierces base easily, turning occasionally, about 30 minutes. Remove artichokes from water and cool.

Gently open top of each artichoke, spreading leaves. Holding artichoke with 1 hand, twist out center cone of leaves with other hand. Reserve cone. Using melon baller, scoop out choke. *(Can be made 1 day ahead. Cover; chill artichokes and cones separately.)*

Place artichokes on plates. Place cones pointed side down in center of artichokes. Spoon 1 tablespoon Roasted Red Pepper Velvet atop each cone. Sprinkle with herbes de Provence. Serve, passing remaining sauce separately.

A dried herb mixture sold at specialty foods stores and some supermarkets. If unavailable, a combination of dried thyme, basil, savory and fennel seeds can be used.

6 SERVINGS

Roasted Red Pepper Velvet

1½ cups plain nonfat yogurt

2 small green onions, cut into1-inch pieces
1 7.25-ounce jar roasted red peppers, well drained, cut into 1-inch pieces
½ teaspoon chopped canned chipotle chilies*
3 tablespoons low-fat mayonnaise
¾ teaspoon herbes de Provence

Set strainer over large bowl. Line strainer with 2 layers of cheesecloth, allowing 4 inches to extend over sides of strainer (do not let strainer touch bottom of bowl). Spoon yogurt into strainer. Fold overhanging cheesecloth over yogurt. Chill overnight (liquid will drain out and yogurt will thicken; discard liquid).

Finely chop green onions in processor. Add half of roasted peppers and chipotle chilies. Process until peppers are finely chopped, scraping down sides of bowl occasionally. Add ½ cup plus 2 tablespoons drained yogurt (reserve any remaining yogurt for another use), mayonnaise and herbes de Provence. Process to blend. Add remaining peppers. Using on/off turns, process until peppers are coarsely chopped. Season with salt and pepper. Transfer to bowl. Chill at least 30 minutes and up to 1 day to blend flavors.

*Chipotle *chilies canned in a spicy tomato sauce, sometimes called adobo, are available at Latin American markets, specialty foods stores and some supermarkets.*

MAKES ABOUT 1½ CUPS

Grilled Clams with Basil-Bacon Salsa

◆ ◆ ◆

10   thick bacon slices

2   cups purchased mild red salsa
½   cup finely chopped fresh basil

6   cups (about) rock salt
48   littleneck clams, scrubbed

Cook 5 bacon slices in medium skillet over medium heat until almost crisp, turning occasionally, about 10 minutes. Transfer to paper towels. Repeat with remaining 5 bacon slices. Chop bacon.

Mix salsa and chopped basil in medium bowl.

Prepare barbecue (medium-high heat). Cover bottom of 2 platters with ¼-inch-thick layer of rock salt. Arrange clams directly on barbecue rack. Cover and grill until clams open, turning occasionally, approximately 8 minutes (discard any clams that do not open). Remove clams from barbecue rack.

Using pot holders to protect hands, twist off and discard top shells of clams. Arrange clams, shell side down, atop salt on platters. Spoon salsa atop clams. Sprinkle with reserved bacon and serve.

8 SERVINGS

A bed of rock salt, which can be purchased in boxes in the baking section of most supermarkets, helps keep the cooked clams in place on the platter—and makes a great presentation.

◆ ◆ ◆

Asparagus with Lemon-Herb Sauce

❖ ❖ ❖

3   cups canned low-salt chicken broth
1½ pounds thin asparagus spears, trimmed

2   tablespoons olive oil (preferably extra virgin)
1¼ cups chopped green onions
⅓   cup minced shallots
1   teaspoon sugar
1   tablespoon minced garlic
1½ tablespoons Dijon mustard
1   tablespoon fresh lemon juice
1   teaspoon minced fresh thyme
½   teaspoon grated lemon peel
½   cup diced seeded red bell peppers

Bring broth to boil in large pot. Add asparagus; cook until crisp-tender, about 4 minutes. Using tongs, transfer asparagus to large bowl of ice water. Reserve 1 cup broth in small bowl. Drain asparagus; pat dry. *(Can be made 1 day ahead. Wrap asparagus in paper towels. Seal in plastic bag. Cover broth. Chill asparagus and broth.)*

Heat 1 tablespoon oil in medium nonstick skillet over medium heat. Add 1 cup green onions, shallots and sugar. Sauté until onions and shallots are tender, about 5 minutes. Add garlic; sauté 2 minutes. Stir in reserved 1 cup broth, 1 tablespoon oil, mustard, lemon juice, thyme and lemon peel. Simmer until slightly thickened and liquid is reduced to 1¼ cups, 5 minutes. Season with salt and pepper. Cool to room temperature. Arrange asparagus on platter. Spoon sauce over. Sprinkle with green onions and peppers.

8 SERVINGS

❖ ❖ ❖

A tangy sauce made with fresh lemon juice, green onions, shallots and mustard turns a classic spring vegetable into a lovely first course.

❖ ❖ ❖

Twice-baked Cheese Soufflés

◆ ◆ ◆

¼ cup dry breadcrumbs
2 tablespoons finely chopped toasted hazelnuts

⅓ cup whole milk
1 tablespoon butter
1 tablespoon all purpose flour
¾ cup grated sharp cheddar cheese
1 large egg yolk

4 large egg whites
1 tablespoon fresh lemon juice
    Pinch of salt

Position rack in center of oven and preheat to 350°F. Mix bread-crumbs and hazelnuts in small bowl. Butter four 8-ounce soufflé dishes or custard cups. Coat sides and bottoms of dishes with breadcrumb mixture. Place dishes in large roasting pan.

Bring milk to boil in heavy large saucepan. Melt butter in heavy small saucepan over medium heat. Add flour and stir until pale golden, about 5 minutes. Whisk in hot milk. Bring to boil, stirring constantly. Reduce heat; simmer 1 minute. Remove from heat. Whisk in ¼ cup cheese and yolk. Cool slightly.

Using electric mixer, beat egg whites, lemon juice and pinch of salt in large bowl until stiff but not dry. Gently fold ¼ of whites into lukewarm cheese mixture to lighten. Fold in remaining whites.

Divide half of soufflé mixture among prepared dishes. Sprin-kle 1 tablespoon cheese over each soufflé. Top with remaining soufflé mixture. Pour enough hot water into roasting pan to come ½ inch up sides of dishes.

Bake soufflés until puffed and tops are golden, about 15 min-utes. Remove dishes from water. Cool 10 minutes. Run knife around sides of soufflés. Gently turn out onto baking sheet. *(Can be made 1 day ahead. Cool. Cover and refrigerate.)*

Sprinkle ¼ cup cheese over soufflés. Bake until heated through, about 8 minutes (or 10 minutes if chilled overnight).

MAKES 4

◆ ◆ ◆

This elegant starter can be par-tially baked, then chilled overnight. Ten minutes before you are ready to eat, simply sprinkle the soufflés with cheese and pop them in the oven until they are heated through and the cheese on top begins to melt.

Mustard-Dill Pancakes with Smoked Salmon and Caviar

◆ ◆ ◆

1¼	cups milk (do not use nonfat)
3	tablespoons Dijon mustard
1	large egg
1	tablespoon yellow mustard seeds
1	cup all purpose flour
2	teaspoons baking powder
3	tablespoons (about) butter, melted
2	tablespoons chopped fresh dill
1	pound thinly sliced smoked salmon
½	cup sour cream
4	ounces caviar

Whisk first 4 ingredients in large bowl to blend. Gradually whisk in flour and baking powder. Stir in 2 tablespoons butter and dill. Cover; let stand 1 hour.

Preheat oven to 250°F. Brush large skillet with butter. Heat over medium heat. Working in batches and brushing with butter, drop batter by tablespoonfuls into skillet, forming 2½-inch rounds. Cook until golden on bottom and bubbles begin to break on surface, about 3 minutes. Turn over; cook until golden, about 2 minutes. Transfer to baking sheet. Keep warm in oven. Top with smoked salmon. Spoon sour cream over. Top with caviar and serve.

8 SERVINGS

◆ ◆ ◆

Here's a modern spin (opposite) on blini, the buckwheat pancakes that are a classic accompaniment to caviar. Topping them with thinly sliced smoked salmon is a delicious way to "gild the lily."

◆ ◆ ◆

Tapenade Dip

◆ ◆ ◆

1	cup pitted Kalamata olives or other brine-cured black olives
1	cup fresh basil leaves
6	canned anchovy fillets
2	tablespoons drained capers
2	garlic cloves, coarsely chopped
1	tablespoon fresh lemon juice
½	cup mayonnaise

Blend all ingredients except mayonnaise in processor until finely chopped. Transfer to small bowl. Mix in mayonnaise.

MAKES ABOUT 1⅓ CUPS

ON A ROLL

Many Asian cuisines feature traditional appetizers composed of savory fillings rolled up inside noodle wrappers. While all are similar in shape and wrapping technique to the spring rolls at right, they vary from country to country in their fillings, in the type and size of noodle wrapper used and in the final preparation method. Here are some common varieties.

◆ Chinese Egg Rolls: deep-fried rolls containing pork and vegetables in an egg-dough wrapper.

◆ Chinese Spring Rolls: lighter deep-fried rolls enclosing shredded vegetables in wrappers made from a flour-and-water dough.

◆ Philippine Lumpia: a wide variety of fillings, from garlicky pork and mushrooms to sweet bananas, fried in thin round flour-and-water or square egg-noodle wrappers.

◆ Thai Spring Rolls: crisply fried packages of garlic-flavored pork, shrimp and noodles in flour-and-water-dough wrappers.

◆ Vietnamese Salad Rolls: uncooked rolls of cold steamed shrimp and pork, lettuce, herbs and rice noodles, in rice-paper wrappers.

◆ Vietnamese Seafood Rolls: crabmeat or shrimp, pork, mushrooms and bean thread noodles deep-fried in very thin rice-paper wrappers.

◆ ◆ ◆

Vietnamese-Style Spring Rolls with Shrimp

◆ ◆ ◆

¼ cup fish sauce (nam pla)*
2 tablespoons thinly sliced green onion
1½ tablespoons fresh lime juice
Pinch of dried crushed red pepper

2 teaspoons olive oil
2 teaspoons minced fresh ginger
16 uncooked medium shrimp, peeled, deveined, halved lengthwise
¼ cup chopped fresh cilantro

4 cups hot water
8 6-inch-diameter Vietnamese spring-roll sheets**

4 small Bibb lettuce leaves, halved
½ cup thin strips green onions
½ cup thin strips seeded peeled cucumber
4 teaspoons minced fresh mint leaves

Mix first 4 ingredients in small bowl. Set dipping sauce aside.

Heat oil in medium skillet over medium-high heat. Add ginger; sauté until fragrant, about 10 seconds. Add shrimp and cilantro; sauté until shrimp are just cooked through, about 1 minute. Remove from heat. Season with salt and pepper.

Pour 4 cups hot water into large bowl. Using tongs, dip 1 spring-roll sheet in water 5 seconds. Remove from water; place on wet towel. Let stand 30 seconds (spring-roll sheet should be soft and pliable; if still stiff, sprinkle with more water).

Place half of 1 lettuce leaf across top third of spring-roll sheet. Arrange 4 shrimp halves on lettuce. Top with 1 tablespoon each of green onions and cucumber. Sprinkle ½ teaspoon mint over filling. Fold sides of spring-roll sheet over ends of filling. Starting at filled side, roll into cylinder. Place on plate. Repeat with remaining spring-roll sheets, lettuce, shrimp, green onions, cucumber and mint. Serve spring rolls with dipping sauce.

*Fish sauce (nam pla) is available at Asian markets and in the Asian foods section of many supermarkets.

**Thin Vietnamese wrappers made from wheat flour and known as banh trang; available at Asian markets.

4 SERVINGS

Scallop Salad with New Potatoes

❖ ❖ ❖

3	tablespoons olive oil
2	tablespoons white wine vinegar
1	teaspoon prepared hot English mustard
1	teaspoon Dijon mustard
½	cup mayonnaise
1	tablespoon whipping cream
3	tablespoons finely chopped fresh chives
8	small red-skinned potatoes
16	medium sea scallops (about 1 pound), halved horizontally
5	ounces mixed baby greens

Whisk 1 tablespoon oil, vinegar and both mustards in medium bowl to blend. Whisk in mayonnaise, then cream. Mix in 2 tablespoons chives. Season vinaigrette to taste with salt and pepper.

Cook potatoes in large saucepan of boiling salted water until just tender, about 12 minutes. Drain potatoes; pat dry with paper towels. Cool completely. Cut each potato crosswise into 4 slices.

Heat remaining 2 tablespoons oil in heavy large skillet over high heat. Add potatoes and sauté until golden, about 2 minutes per side. Using slotted spoon, transfer potatoes to plate. Add scallops to same skillet and sauté until just cooked through, 1 minute per side.

Toss mixed greens in large bowl with enough vinaigrette to coat. Season with salt and pepper. Spoon salad onto plates. Arrange scallops and potatoes atop salad. Drizzle remaining vinaigrette around scallops and potatoes. Sprinkle with remaining chives.

4 SERVINGS

❖ ❖ ❖

Red potatoes and sea scallops are both sautéed, then served warm atop a bed of mixed baby greens. This makes an attractive first course for an elegant dinner party.

❖ ❖ ❖

Fish Cakes with Shrimp and Smoked Salmon

◆ ◆ ◆

1	pound russet potatoes, peeled, cut into ½-inch pieces
1	6-ounce orange roughy fillet
¼	pound bay shrimp, chopped
3	ounces smoked salmon, chopped
½	cup chopped green onions
¼	cup chopped fresh dill
2	teaspoons grated lemon peel
2	cups fresh breadcrumbs from French bread
5	tablespoons (about) vegetable oil
	Lemon wedges

Steam potatoes until tender, about 10 minutes. Transfer potatoes to large bowl and mash. Steam fish until cooked through, about 10 minutes. Transfer fish to plate; cool 5 minutes. Flake fish and add to potatoes. Mix in shrimp, smoked salmon, green onions, dill and lemon peel. Season to taste with salt and pepper. Using about ⅓ cupful at a time, shape fish mixture into 12 balls; flatten each into ½-inch-thick cake. Place breadcrumbs in shallow bowl. Coat each cake with breadcrumbs, pressing to adhere.

Heat 3 tablespoons oil in heavy large skillet over medium heat. Working in batches, sauté fish cakes until brown and heated through, adding more oil as needed, about 3 minutes per side. Divide fish cakes among 4 plates. Serve with lemon wedges.

4 SERVINGS

Taking their inspiration from crab cakes, these fish cakes combine orange roughy, shrimp and smoked salmon, all held together with mashed potatoes. After a breadcrumb coating, they cook up in just minutes.

Spiced Nuts

◆ ◆ ◆

2	tablespoons olive oil
½	teaspoon ground ginger
½	teaspoon curry powder
¼	teaspoon cayenne pepper
2	tablespoons sugar
1	tablespoon honey
¾	cup walnut halves
¾	cup pecan halves

Line baking sheet with foil. Lightly oil foil. Heat 2 tablespoons oil in large nonstick skillet over medium heat. Add ginger, curry powder and cayenne pepper; sauté until fragrant, about 5 seconds. Stir in sugar and honey. Add nuts. Stir until honey mixture caramelizes and nuts are well coated, about 6 minutes.

Transfer nut mixture to prepared baking sheet. Working quickly, separate nuts with spoon. Sprinkle with salt. Cool. *(Can be made 3 days ahead. Store in airtight container at room temperature.)*

MAKES 1½ CUPS

Artichokes Stuffed with Lemon-Garlic Breadcrumbs

◆ ◆ ◆

2	cups fresh breadcrumbs from crustless French bread
¼	cup olive oil
2	tablespoons fresh lemon juice
1	tablespoon chopped fresh oregano
3	garlic cloves, minced
1	teaspoon grated lemon peel
6	medium artichokes, trimmed, left whole, chokes removed
2	tablespoons (¼ stick) butter, cut into 6 pieces
½	cup (or more) water
	Lemon wedges

Preheat oven to 400°F. Mix breadcrumbs and oil in medium bowl. Spread mixture on large rimmed baking sheet. Bake until golden on edges, stirring occasionally, about 10 minutes. Transfer to large bowl. Mix in lemon juice, oregano, garlic and lemon peel. Season to taste with salt and pepper.

Drain artichokes. Gently pull leaves outward from center until leaves open slightly. Fill artichoke cavities with bread stuffing. Pack stuffing between leaves. Place artichokes in 13 x 9 x 2-inch glass baking dish. Dot tops with butter. Pour ½ cup water into dish.

Cover dish with foil; bake until wooden skewer pierces artichokes easily, adding more water as necessary, about 40 minutes. Remove foil. Continue baking until tops are golden, about 20 minutes. Serve artichokes with lemon wedges.

6 SERVINGS

AN UNCOMMON VEGETABLE

The artichoke we know and love is actually the edible bud of the spike-leaved perennial plant, a member of the thistle group of the sunflower family. More than two-thirds of the domestic crop is grown around the small, central California town of Castroville, where artichokes have been sprouting since 1922 when several Italian immigrant families planted the first crops. Now, the six thousand acres surrounding the town come to life every spring when it's time to harvest the 'chokes—and celebrate this annual event. If you're planning an artichoke celebration, here's a simple way to prepare the vegetable.

Cut off the top half of the artichoke and the stem and discard. Starting at the base, bend the tough outer leaves back and snap off where they break naturally, leaving the tender inner leaves. Using a small sharp knife, trim the outside of the base until no dark green areas remain. Rub the trimmed area with a lemon half. If leaving the artichoke whole (as in the recipe at left), scoop out the fibrous choke and small purple-tipped leaves, using a spoon. Rub the exposed areas with a lemon half. Place the prepared artichoke in lemon water until ready to use or up to two hours.

◆ ◆ ◆

Goat Cheese Ravioli with Basil

◆ ◆ ◆

1	large garlic clove
1	5.5-ounce log soft fresh goat cheese (such as Montrachet)
⅔	cup fresh ricotta cheese
½	cup chopped fresh basil
2	large egg yolks
24	egg roll or spring roll wrappers*
1	egg, beaten to blend
	Extra-virgin olive oil
	Parmesan cheese, shaved
	Fresh basil sprigs

Finely chop garlic in processor. Add goat cheese, ricotta and chopped basil and blend until smooth. Season filling to taste with salt and pepper. Blend in egg yolks.

Using 4-inch round cookie cutter, cut out 1 round from each egg roll wrapper. Place scant 1 tablespoon filling in center of each round. Brush edges of wrappers with beaten egg. Fold in half; press edges to seal. *(Can be made 6 hours ahead. Arrange on floured baking sheet. Cover with plastic wrap; chill.)*

Working in batches, cook ravioli in large pot of boiling salted water until just tender, stirring occasionally, about 2 minutes per batch. Using slotted spoon, transfer ravioli to large shallow bowl.

Drizzle olive oil over ravioli. Sprinkle with shaved Parmesan. Garnish with basil sprigs. Serve ravioli immediately.

*Available at Asian markets and many supermarkets.

6 SERVINGS

If time allows, you might go all out and make the pasta dough for the ravioli. Otherwise, egg roll wrappers are a quick and easy substitute.

◆ ◆ ◆

Red Caviar Dip

◆ ◆ ◆

1	cup sour cream
2	green onions, very thinly sliced
1	tablespoon fresh lemon juice
1	tablespoon plus 1 teaspoon chopped fresh chives
¼	cup plus 3 tablespoons salmon caviar, drained, gently rinsed

Mix sour cream, green onions, lemon juice and 1 tablespoon chives in medium bowl. Gently fold in ¼ cup caviar. Transfer to serving bowl. *(Cover and refrigerate at least 6 hours and up to 1 day.)* Sprinkle with remaining caviar and chives.

MAKES ABOUT 1 CUP

Spinach and Red Pepper Crostini

◆ ◆ ◆

2	teaspoons plus 2 tablespoons olive oil
½	red bell pepper, cut into matchstick-size strips
1	10-ounce package fresh spinach, stemmed
1	teaspoon minced garlic
¼	cup chopped prosciutto
1	tablespoon whipping cream
12	½-inch-thick slices cut from French-bread baguette
6	tablespoons freshly grated Parmesan cheese

Heat 1 teaspoon oil in large skillet over medium heat. Add bell pepper; sauté until crisp-tender, 8 minutes. Transfer to bowl.

Heat same skillet over high heat. Add spinach and sauté 2 minutes. Reduce heat to medium and sauté until tender, 2 minutes longer. Cool in skillet. Transfer to work surface; chop spinach.

Heat 1 teaspoon oil in same skillet over medium heat. Add garlic and sauté until fragrant, about 30 seconds. Add prosciutto and sauté 30 seconds. Add chopped spinach. Sauté 2 minutes. Season to taste with salt and pepper. Remove from heat. Mix in cream.

Preheat broiler. Arrange bread slices on large baking sheet. Broil until lightly toasted. Turn bread slices over. Brush top of bread slices with remaining 2 tablespoons oil. Broil until lightly toasted. Cool. *(Can be made 8 hours ahead. Cover spinach mixture and bell pepper strips separately; chill. Store toasts airtight at room temperature.)*

Spoon generous 1 tablespoon spinach mixture atop each toast. Arrange bell pepper strips atop toasts. Sprinkle with Parmesan. Broil crostini until cheese bubbles and spinach mixture is hot, about 2 minutes. Transfer crostini to plate and serve.

MAKES 12

The *crostini* can be assembled two hours ahead of time and then popped under the broiler just before serving.

◆ ◆ ◆

Asparagus and Leek Risotto with Prosciutto

◆ ◆ ◆

1   pound asparagus spears, tough ends trimmed, cut diagonally into ½-inch pieces
5   cups canned low-salt chicken broth

3   tablespoons butter
1   tablespoon olive oil
1   cup thinly sliced leek (white and pale green parts only)
1½ cups arborio rice or medium-grain white rice
½   cup dry white wine
2   ounces prosciutto, minced (about ¼ cup)
3   tablespoons freshly grated Parmesan cheese
2   tablespoons chopped fresh parsley

Cook asparagus in large pot of boiling salted water until crisp-tender, about 2 minutes. Drain. Transfer asparagus to bowl of ice water to cool. Drain. Bring broth to boil in medium saucepan. Reduce heat to very low; cover and keep broth warm.

Meanwhile, melt butter with oil in heavy large saucepan over medium heat. Add leek and sauté until tender, about 5 minutes. Add rice and stir 2 minutes. Add wine and simmer until absorbed, stirring constantly, about 5 minutes. Add ½ cup hot chicken broth. Reduce heat and simmer until absorbed, stirring frequently. Add remaining broth ½ cup at a time, allowing broth to be absorbed before adding more and stirring frequently until rice is just tender and mixture is creamy, about 30 minutes. Add asparagus and stir until heated through, about 2 minutes. Remove from heat. Stir in prosciutto, Parmesan and parsley. Season with salt and pepper.

4 SERVINGS

Risotto is traditionally made with *arborio*, a high-starch Italian rice that contributes to the creamy texture of the dish. If arborio rice isn't readily available, medium-grain white rice can successfully be used instead.

◆ ◆ ◆

Orange-marinated Olives

◆ ◆ ◆

1   cup Kalamata olives or other black or green brine-cured olives
¼   cup fresh orange juice
¼   cup olive oil
2   tablespoons very thin matchstick-size strips orange peel
2   garlic cloves, very thinly sliced
½   teaspoon (or more) dried crushed red pepper

Mix first 5 ingredients in small bowl. Season to taste with red pepper and salt. Cover and refrigerate overnight. *(Can be prepared 4 days ahead. Keep refrigerated.)*

MAKES 1 CUP

Lemony White Bean Skordalia with Grill-toasted Pita

◆ ◆ ◆

1   cup (about 6½ ounces) dried Great Northern beans

1   tablespoon chopped garlic
⅓   cup fresh lemon juice
¼   cup tahini (sesame seed paste)*
¼   cup olive oil (preferably extra-virgin)
¼   cup finely chopped fresh parsley
3   tablespoons finely chopped fresh mint

6   6-inch-diameter pita bread rounds, cut into wedges

Place beans in heavy medium saucepan. Add enough water to cover by 2 inches. Let stand at room temperature overnight.

Drain soaked beans. Return to saucepan. Add enough cold water to cover beans by 2 inches. Bring to boil. Reduce heat to medium. Cover partially and simmer until beans are very tender, stirring occasionally, about 1 hour 10 minutes. Drain beans thoroughly, reserving ¼ cup cooking liquid.

Place beans, 2 tablespoons reserved cooking liquid and garlic in processor. Process until beans are coarsely chopped. Add lemon juice, tahini and oil. Process until smooth, scraping down sides of bowl occasionally and thinning with more cooking liquid by teaspoonfuls if necessary. Season with salt and pepper. Transfer to small bowl. Stir in parsley and mint. *(Can be made 1 day ahead. Cover; chill.)*

Prepare barbecue (medium-high heat). Grill pita wedges until beginning to brown, about 1 minute per side. Transfer pita wedges to basket and serve with skordalia.

*Available at Middle Eastern and natural foods stores.

4 SERVINGS

◆ ◆ ◆

Skordalia is a classic Greek spread made with potatoes. The use of white beans in their place—plus the addition of tahini, along with lots of fresh mint and parsley—transforms the easy appetizer into a whole new treat.

◆ ◆ ◆

Leek and Orange Soup

◆ ◆ ◆

1½ cups chilled whipping cream
1   tablespoon Cointreau or other orange liqueur
2   teaspoons finely grated orange peel

¼   cup (½ stick) butter
5   cups chopped leeks (white and pale green parts only; about 4 large)
1½ pounds russet potatoes, peeled, cut into ½-inch pieces
2   teaspoons chopped fresh tarragon
5   cups (or more) chicken stock or canned low-salt chicken broth

Fresh chervil leaves

Using electric mixer, beat ½ cup cream, Cointreau and orange peel in large bowl until firm peaks form. Cover and refrigerate orange cream up to 8 hours.

Melt butter in heavy large pot over medium-high heat. Add leeks and sauté until translucent, about 10 minutes. Add potatoes and tarragon; stir 2 minutes. Add 5 cups stock. Bring mixture to boil. Reduce heat to low, cover partially and simmer until potatoes are very tender, about 25 minutes. Mix in remaining 1 cup cream.

Working in batches, puree soup in blender until smooth. Return to pot. Thin with more stock, if desired. Season with salt and

◆ ◆ ◆

This velvety leek and potato soup is seasoned with fresh tarragon and topped with orange-flavored whipped cream, which is browned under the broiler just before serving. If you don't have broilerproof bowls, you can eliminate this last step.

◆ ◆ ◆

pepper. *(Can be made 8 hours ahead. Chill until cold, then cover. Rewarm soup over medium heat before continuing.)*

Preheat broiler. Ladle soup into 6 broilerproof bowls. Spoon dollop of orange cream atop each serving. Broil until cream begins to brown, about 1 minute. Garnish with chervil leaves and serve.

6 SERVINGS

Toasted Noodle Soup with Chipotle Chilies

◆ ◆ ◆

Here, *fideos* noodles, very thin pasta strands similar to vermicelli, are sautéed first, which enriches the flavor of this tomato soup.

◆ ◆ ◆

1½   pounds ripe plum tomatoes, coarsely chopped
2   cups coarsely chopped red onions
½   cup water
6   garlic cloves, peeled

2   tablespoons (¼ stick) butter
2   tablespoons olive oil
8   ounces fideos noodles,* broken into 1-inch pieces
2   teaspoons chopped canned chipotle chilies**
5   cups (or more) chicken stock or canned low-salt chicken broth

1   avocado, peeled, pitted, cut into thin wedges
¾   cup chopped fresh cilantro
      Lime wedges

Puree tomatoes, chopped red onions, ½ cup water and garlic cloves in blender until smooth. Set aside.

Melt butter with olive oil in heavy large saucepan over medium heat. Add noodles and sauté until golden brown, about 6 minutes. Add chipotle chilies and sauté 2 minutes longer. Add tomato mixture and 5 cups chicken stock. Simmer 20 minutes to blend flavors, stirring occasionally. Thin soup with more stock if desired. Season soup to taste with salt and pepper.

Ladle soup into bowls. Serve immediately with avocado, chopped cilantro and lime wedges.

*Fideos *noodles are available at Latin American markets and some supermarkets. The Italian version, which is called* fedelini, *is available in many Italian markets.*

**Chipotle *chilies canned in a spicy tomato sauce, sometimes called adobo, are available at Latin American markets, specialty foods stores and some supermarkets.*

6 SERVINGS

Cream of Onion Soup

◆ ◆ ◆

2   tablespoons (¼ stick) butter
5   cups sliced onions (about 1¼ pounds)
2   large garlic cloves, peeled, halved
5   cups canned low-salt chicken broth
1   7- to 8-ounce russet potato, peeled, cut into ¾-inch pieces

½   cup whipping cream
1   tablespoon dry Sherry
1   teaspoon minced fresh thyme
    Minced fresh chives

Melt butter in heavy large pot over medium heat. Add onions and sauté until very tender and pale golden, about 25 minutes. Add garlic and stir 1 minute. Add chicken broth and potato and bring to boil. Reduce heat; cover and simmer until potato is very tender, about 25 minutes. Cool soup slightly.

Working in batches, puree soup in blender. Return to pot. Stir in cream, Sherry and thyme. Simmer about 10 minutes. Season with salt and pepper. *(Can be made 2 days ahead; chill. Bring to simmer before serving.)* Sprinkle with chives.

6 SERVINGS

Yellow Bell Pepper Soup

◆ ◆ ◆

10   large yellow bell peppers (about 4 pounds), cut into 2-inch pieces
2   tablespoons olive oil

4½   cups (or more) canned low-salt chicken broth
1   cup half and half
1   teaspoon sugar

    Italian parsley sprigs

Preheat oven to 400°F. Line 2 large baking sheets with heavy-duty foil. Toss bell peppers with oil in large bowl. Arrange in single layer on baking sheets. Roast until peppers are tender and beginning to brown, stirring occasionally, about 50 minutes.

This recipe for onion soup—a bistro classic—is enriched with cream and a touch of Sherry. Fresh chives are sprinkled over each serving for an elegant finish.

◆ ◆ ◆

Transfer peppers to heavy large saucepan. Add 4½ cups broth. Boil 8 minutes to blend flavors. Cool slightly. Working in batches, puree mixture in blender. Return to saucepan. Mix in half and half and sugar. Thin soup with more broth if desired. Season with salt and pepper. *(Can be made 1 day ahead. Cover and refrigerate. Rewarm over medium heat before continuing.)*

Spoon soup into bowls. Garnish with parsley sprigs and serve.

6 SERVINGS

Curried Lentil Soup

◆ ◆ ◆

2	tablespoons olive oil
1	large onion, chopped
1	8-ounce russet potato, peeled, chopped
1	large carrot, peeled, chopped
2	tablespoons curry powder
¼	teaspoon cayenne pepper
3	14½-ounce cans low-salt chicken broth
1	28-ounce can diced tomatoes in juice
2	cups lentils (about 12 ounces), rinsed, drained

Heat oil in heavy large pot over medium-high heat. Add onion, potato and carrot and sauté until vegetables begin to soften, about 5 minutes. Mix in curry powder and cayenne and stir until fragrant, about 30 seconds. Add broth, tomatoes with juices and lentils and bring to boil. Cover pot, reduce heat to medium-low and simmer until lentils are very tender, about 45 minutes. Season soup to taste with salt and pepper. *(Can be made up to 2 days ahead. Refrigerate until cold; cover and keep refrigerated. Before serving, rewarm soup over low heat.)*

6 TO 8 SERVINGS

THE IDEAL STOCKPOT

A stockpot is useful for a variety of cooking tasks, from making stock and soup to cooking chili and pasta, even braising. But with so many shapes and sizes available, what kind of stockpot to purchase can be bewildering.

Good-quality stockpots range in price from about $50 (made of stainless steel) to upwards of $200 (made of copper and lined with nickel). Look for one with sturdy, heatproof handles and a heavy bottom, which will prevent burning.

What size to buy? Just how big the pot should be depends on several factors: *your* size (a large stockpot can be very heavy to lift when fully loaded); the size of the job (chicken soup for four or chili for 20); and the size of your storage space (of which there never seems to be enough).

We asked *Bon Appétit* Senior Food Editor Sarah Tenaglia what size is best. "The twelve-quart is probably the most useful-size stockpot to have," she says, "especially if you entertain for larger groups." But she also thought that the eight-quart pot was a practical choice if you don't usually cook for a lot of people. Still not sure what to do? Take Tenaglia's advice: "Buy both."

◆ ◆ ◆

Shrimp Broth with Lemongrass, Chili and Ginger

◆ ◆ ◆

¾   pound uncooked large shrimp

6   14½-ounce cans low-salt chicken broth
1   cup finely chopped carrot
⅓   cup thinly sliced fresh lemongrass
3   tablespoons finely chopped fresh ginger
2   tablespoons minced garlic

1½   tablespoons finely chopped fresh basil
1½   tablespoons finely chopped fresh mint
1½   tablespoons finely chopped cilantro
1   small serrano chili, stemmed, thinly sliced into rounds
1½   teaspoons fresh lime juice

6   thin lime slices

Peel and devein shrimp; reserve shells. Halve shrimp lengthwise. Transfer shrimp to small bowl. Cover and chill.

Combine reserved shrimp shells, broth and next 4 ingredients in large pot. Bring to boil. Reduce heat; simmer uncovered 20 minutes to blend flavors, stirring and skimming surface occasionally. *(Can be made 1 day ahead. Cover; chill.)*

Strain broth into large bowl, pressing on solids with back of spoon to release as much liquid as possible; discard solids. Return broth to pot. Bring to simmer. Remove from heat. Add shrimp, herbs, chili and lime juice. Cover and let stand until shrimp are opaque, stirring once, about 2 minutes.

Ladle into bowls. Garnish with lime slices and serve.

6 SERVINGS

Combining spicy and tangy flavors, this soup is exotic without being complex. Look for lemongrass—an important ingredient in Thai cooking—at Asian markets and in the produce section of some supermarkets.

◆ ◆ ◆

Ideal for a large party, this recipe serves 12 and can be prepared a day ahead (rewarm it just before sitting down to eat). It's also simple to make.

◆ ◆ ◆

Carrot Soup with Caraway and Cumin

◆ ◆ ◆

14	cups canned low-salt chicken broth
2½	pounds carrots, sliced
4	cups chopped onions
2½	teaspoons ground cumin
2	teaspoons caraway seeds, crushed
1	teaspoon garlic powder
¼	cup fresh lime juice

Fresh cilantro leaves

Combine broth, carrots, onions, cumin, caraway and garlic powder in large pot. Bring to boil over high heat. Reduce heat to medium-low, cover pot and simmer until carrots are very tender, about 1 hour. Mix in fresh lime juice.

Working in small batches, puree soup in blender until smooth. Season to taste with salt and pepper. *(Can be prepared 1 day ahead. Cover and refrigerate. Rewarm soup before serving.)*

Ladle soup into bowls. Garnish with cilantro leaves and serve.

12 SERVINGS

ALL ABOUT GREEN ONIONS

Sometimes referred to as a spring onion, more often as a scallion, the green onion is an allium with almost as many names as it has uses. It's also occasionally called a young leek—something it's not, despite similarities in appearance: Both are tall, with a dark green top and bright white lower portion that flares slightly at the root. But where the leek is mild, even slightly sweet-tasting, the green onion packs a punch of oniony flavor.

Green onions probably originated in central Asia and were then carried along trade routes to east Asia and Europe. From Europe, the onions migrated with the conquistadors to the Americas. Green onions remain a much-used ingredient in Mexico and are still popular in east Asia. Korea grows the most, with Japan and China next. The bulk of our crop comes from California's coastal valleys.

In addition to adding terrific flavor to a variety of dishes, green onions can dress up a plate. To make green onion "brushes," remove the root and the green top from several green onions, then score the bottoms with a knife. Let the onions soak overnight in cold water, which causes the bottoms to flare and resemble paintbrushes.

◆ ◆ ◆

Coconut Chicken Soup

◆ ◆ ◆

2	14-ounce cans light unsweetened coconut milk*
3	cups canned chicken broth
2	cups thinly sliced mushrooms
6	tablespoons finely chopped lemongrass*
¼	cup fish sauce (nam pla)*
2	tablespoons minced fresh ginger
1	serrano chili, sliced into rounds
2	teaspoons chili-garlic sauce*
8	skinless boneless chicken thighs, thinly sliced
½	cup thinly sliced green onions
¼	cup thinly sliced fresh basil
3	tablespoons fresh lime juice

Combine first 8 ingredients in large saucepan. Bring to boil. Reduce heat; cover and simmer 10 minutes to blend flavors. Add chicken; simmer until cooked through, about 5 minutes. Mix in green onions, basil and lime juice. Serve immediately.

*Available at Asian markets and many supermarkets.

6 SERVINGS

Tomato and Basil Soup

◆ ◆ ◆

2	tablespoons olive oil
1	cup chopped peeled carrot
1	cup chopped onion
1	cup chopped celery
1	tablespoon chopped fresh thyme or 1 teaspoon dried
2	teaspoons minced garlic
1	bay leaf
1	28-ounce can diced tomatoes in juice
1	14½- to 16-ounce can diced tomatoes in juice
1¾	cups vegetable stock or canned vegetable broth
½	cup whipping cream
4	tablespoons chopped fresh basil
1	plum tomato, seeded, chopped

Heat 2 tablespoons olive oil in heavy large saucepan over medium heat. Add chopped carrot, onion and celery; sauté until beginning to soften, about 5 minutes. Mix in thyme, garlic and bay leaf. Add all canned tomatoes with their juices and vegetable stock; simmer 20 minutes. Add whipping cream; simmer 5 minutes. Mix in 3 tablespoons chopped fresh basil. Remove bay leaf. Working in batches, puree soup in blender. Transfer to large saucepan. Season soup with salt and pepper. *(Can be made 1 day ahead. Cover; chill.)*

Bring soup to simmer. Ladle into bowls. Sprinkle with chopped tomato and remaining 1 tablespoon chopped basil.

6 SERVINGS

Butternut Squash Soup with Ginger

◆ ◆ ◆

2	butternut squash (about 4¾ pounds total), halved lengthwise, seeded
2	tablespoons vegetable oil
2	cups thinly sliced onion
1	tablespoon golden brown sugar
2	teaspoons minced fresh ginger
2	garlic cloves, coarsely chopped
½	cinnamon stick
5	cups (or more) canned low-salt chicken broth

Chopped fresh parsley

Preheat oven to 375°F. Oil baking sheet. Place squash, cut side down, on baking sheet. Bake until squash is very soft, about 50 minutes. Using paring knife, remove peel from squash; discard peel. Cut squash into 2-inch pieces. Set aside.

Heat oil in heavy large pot over medium-low heat. Mix in onion, brown sugar, ginger, garlic and cinnamon. Cover pot and cook until onion is tender, about 15 minutes. Add squash and 5 cups chicken broth. Bring to boil. Reduce heat to medium-low. Cover and simmer 10 minutes. Discard cinnamon.

Working in batches, puree soup in blender. *(Can be prepared 1 day ahead. Cool slightly. Cover and refrigerate.)* Return soup to pot. Season with salt and pepper. Bring to simmer, thinning soup with more broth if necessary. Ladle into bowls. Sprinkle with parsley.

8 SERVINGS

◆ ◆ ◆

Cinnamon, brown sugar, ginger and garlic add complexity to this rich, creamy soup. Make it a day ahead and simply rewarm before serving.

◆ ◆ ◆

Corn Bisque with Rosemary

◆ ◆ ◆

This simple and delicious soup gets a hint of spiciness from cayenne pepper. Corn kernels and chopped red pepper add texture and color.

◆ ◆ ◆

4	tablespoons (½ stick) butter
2	cups chopped onions
½	cup diced carrot
½	cup diced celery
7½	cups frozen corn kernels, thawed, drained
1	teaspoon dried rosemary
¼	teaspoon cayenne pepper
6	cups canned low-salt chicken broth
1	cup half and half
1	red bell pepper, chopped

Melt 3 tablespoons butter in heavy large pot over medium-high heat. Add onions, carrot and celery and sauté 3 minutes. Add 5½ cups corn, rosemary and cayenne and sauté 2 minutes. Add broth and bring to boil. Reduce heat to medium-low; simmer uncovered until vegetables are tender and liquid is slightly reduced, 30 minutes.

Working in batches, puree soup in blender. Return to pot. Mix in half and half and 2 cups corn. Season with salt and pepper.

Melt remaining 1 tablespoon butter in heavy large skillet over medium-high heat. Add bell pepper and sauté until almost tender, about 5 minutes. Stir bell pepper into soup. *(Can be prepared 1 day ahead. Cover and refrigerate.)*

Bring soup to simmer. Ladle into bowls and serve.

10 SERVINGS

Chilled Beet, Orange and Dill Soup

◆ ◆ ◆

3   15-ounce cans julienne beets, drained, ¾ cup liquid reserved
1½   cups fresh orange juice
1½   cups reduced-fat (2%) buttermilk
3   tablespoons chopped fresh dill

1½   cups finely diced unpeeled English hothouse cucumber
       (about ½ large)
       Additional chopped fresh dill

Combine half of beets, half of reserved beet liquid and half of orange juice in blender. Blend until smooth. Blend in half of buttermilk and 1½ tablespoons chopped dill. Transfer to large bowl. Repeat with remaining beets, beet liquid, orange juice, buttermilk and 1½ tablespoons dill. Season with salt and pepper. Chill at least 3 hours. *(Can be made 2 days ahead. Cover and keep chilled.)*

Garnish soup with cucumber and additional dill.

8 SERVINGS

◆ ◆ ◆

This pretty soup is easy to make with canned julienne beets. Low-fat buttermilk provides a creamy texture and a nice tang without adding a lot of calories, fat or cholesterol.

◆ ◆ ◆

Spicy Gazpacho

◆ ◆ ◆

2   cups diced seeded peeled cucumber
1   cup chopped celery
1   cup chopped green onions
1   4-ounce can chopped mild green chilies

3   14½-ounce cans diced tomatoes in juice
1   slice white bread, torn into pieces
¼   cup olive oil
¼   cup drained capers
2   tablespoons red wine vinegar
1   tablespoon chili powder
2   garlic cloves

Place 1 cup cucumber, ½ cup celery, ½ cup green onions and half of chilies in small bowl and reserve.

Working in batches, coarsely puree remaining cucumber, celery, green onions, chilies and next 7 ingredients in blender. Pour into large bowl. Mix in reserved vegetables. Season with salt and pepper. Chill at least 6 hours and up to 1 day.

6 TO 8 SERVINGS

GIVE IT A WHIRL

Smoothies are great for people on the go. They're delicious, refreshing, satisfying and healthful—not to mention quick and easy to make. All you need is a blender, some fruit and milk, yogurt or juice. Try one of the recipes featured at right or create your own concoction, using these tips.

◆ For a single serving, an easy rule of thumb is to combine 2 medium fruits and ¾ cup yogurt.

◆ For a thick smoothie with a texture similar to ice cream, try using frozen yogurt instead of the refrigerated kind. For a lighter smoothie, use just pureed fruit, juice and ice cubes.

◆ Peel and dice bananas and freeze them in small plastic bags. They make a delicious addition to smoothies, as do frozen berries.

◆ If a smoothie tastes too tart, just whirl in some added honey or sugar (white or brown) to taste.

◆ Wheat germ or protein powder make great add-ins for a smoothie at breakfast—or anytime you need an energy boost, for that matter.

◆ ◆ ◆

Very Berry Smoothie

◆ ◆ ◆

1¾	cups low-fat blueberry yogurt	
¼	cup grape juice	
1½	cups frozen blueberries	
1	cup frozen blackberries	

Combine blueberry yogurt and grape juice in blender. Add blueberries and blackberries. Blend until mixture is thick and smooth. Pour smoothie into 2 glasses and serve immediately.

2 SERVINGS

Tropical-Blend Smoothie

◆ ◆ ◆

1   very ripe banana, sliced
1   cup diced pitted peeled fresh mango (from about 1 small)
1   cup diced peeled fresh pineapple

1   cup unsweetened pineapple juice
½   cup canned light unsweetened coconut milk*
1   teaspoon fresh lime juice

Arrange banana, mango and pineapple in single layer on baking sheet. Cover and freeze until fruit is frozen solid, about 2 hours.

Combine pineapple juice, coconut milk and lime juice in blender. Add frozen fruit. Blend until mixture is thick and smooth. Pour into glasses and serve immediately.

*Available at Indian, Southeast Asian and Latin American markets and also at many supermarkets.

2 SERVINGS

ALL ABOUT MARSHMALLOWS

All-American though marshmallows may seem, they are among the world's oldest sweets. Their use stretches back some four millennia to ancient Egypt, where the light, fluffy confections were deemed food for gods.

Until a century and a half ago, marshmallows were made from the root of the marsh mallow, a plant that grows wild in marshlands—hence the name, which derives from the Old English *merscmealve*. The plant's roots contain a sap that was the basis for the candy. Nineteenth-century French confectioners developed a way to make a similar sweet using beaten egg whites, sugar syrup and gelatin.

Sold in pieces commonly measuring about one inch, or in miniature pieces, marshmallows are usually pure white and neutral-tasting, although colored and flavored varieties also exist. They are most often enjoyed straight from the package; as a garnish for hot chocolate; or toasted until golden brown and combined with chocolate and graham crackers to make S'mores. Marshmallows are also included as an ingredient in cooked confections, frosting, or baked goods; and they traditionally top baked sweet potatoes at Thanksgiving.

◆ ◆ ◆

Milk Chocolate and Orange Hot Chocolate

◆ ◆ ◆

⅓ cup chilled whipping cream
1 teaspoon (packed) dark brown sugar

4½ cups milk
4 large oranges

9 ounces good-quality milk chocolate (such as Lindt or Ghirardelli), chopped
2 tablespoons unsweetened cocoa powder
   Milk chocolate curls (optional)
   Orange peel twists (optional)

Whisk cream and brown sugar in medium bowl until stiff peaks form. Cover and refrigerate whipped cream.

Pour milk into heavy large saucepan. Using vegetable peeler, remove peel (orange part only) from 4 oranges. Add peel to milk (reserve oranges for another use). Bring milk mixture to simmer over medium-high heat. Remove from heat. Cover; steep 30 minutes.

Strain milk mixture into large bowl, pressing on solids to remove liquid. Return milk to same saucepan. Bring to simmer over medium-high heat. Add chopped chocolate and cocoa powder;

whisk until melted and smooth. Simmer 1 minute, whisking constantly. Ladle hot chocolate into 4 ceramic cups or mugs. Top each with dollop of whipped cream. Sprinkle with chocolate curls and garnish with orange peel twists, if desired.

4 SERVINGS

Ultra-Rich Hot Chocolate

◆ ◆ ◆

4   cups milk
¼   cup unsweetened cocoa powder
¼   cup sugar
4   ounces bittersweet (not unsweetened) or
     semisweet chocolate, chopped
     Pinch of salt
     Miniature marshmallows

Bring milk, cocoa powder and sugar to simmer in heavy large saucepan over medium-high heat, whisking frequently. Add chocolate; whisk until melted and smooth. Add salt; bring to simmer, whisking constantly until frothy. Ladle hot chocolate into 4 mugs. Sprinkle with marshmallows and serve.

4 SERVINGS

Irish Coffee

◆ ◆ ◆

¾   cup chilled whipping cream
1¾   cups plus 2 tablespoons Irish whiskey
10   tablespoons (packed) dark brown sugar
7½   cups freshly brewed strong coffee
     Grated semisweet chocolate

Whisk cream in large bowl until slightly thickened. Place 3 tablespoons whiskey and 1 tablespoon brown sugar in each of ten 8- to 10-ounce mugs. Pour ¾ cup coffee into each mug. Top each with dollop of cream; sprinkle with chocolate.

10 SERVINGS

Pimm's Cup

Ice cubes
4 strawberries
4 lemon slices
4 lime slices
4 orange slices
12 tablespoons Pimm's No. 1 Cup*
2 cups chilled lemon-lime soda
4 cucumber wedges
4 fresh mint sprigs

Fill four 8- to 10-ounce glasses with ice cubes. Divide fruit among glasses. Pour 3 tablespoons Pimm's No. 1 Cup and ½ cup soda into each glass. Garnish with cucumber and mint.

A blend of gin, liqueurs and fruit extracts; available at some liquor stores and specialty foods stores.

4 SERVINGS

The fruity gin-based liquor Pimm's No. 1 Cup was created in 1840 by London oyster bar proprietor James Pimm. These days, the Pimm's Cup cocktail remains the quintessential British fair-weather drink. It almost always comes with a garnish of cucumber; opinion varies, though, on whether to serve the drink over ice, crushed or otherwise.

Rum and Lime Punch

¾ cup water
½ cup sugar

1 cup dark rum
¾ cup fresh lime juice
5 tablespoons grenadine
¼ teaspoon Angostura bitters
⅛ teaspoon ground nutmeg
Ice cubes
Lime slices

Stir ¾ cup water and sugar in small saucepan over low heat until sugar dissolves. Bring to simmer. Remove from heat; cool.

Mix sugar syrup, rum, lime juice, grenadine, bitters and nutmeg in pitcher. Fill 4 tall glasses with ice. Pour rum punch over. Garnish each glass with lime slice and serve.

4 SERVINGS

Minted Vodka Lemonade

◆ ◆ ◆

1   cup (packed) mint leaves, chopped
⅔   cup sugar
1   cup fresh lemon juice
1½ cups vodka

    Crushed ice
    Fresh mint sprigs

Combine chopped mint and sugar in large bowl. Stir in fresh lemon juice and vodka. Cover vodka mixture and refrigerate for at least 30 minutes and up to 2 hours.

Strain mixture into pitcher. Fill six 6- to 8-ounce glasses with crushed ice. Pour mixture over. Garnish with mint sprigs.

6 SERVINGS

Watermelon and Strawberry Margaritas

◆ ◆ ◆

3   cups (packed) frozen chopped seeded watermelon
1   cup (packed) frozen quartered unsweetened strawberries
7   tablespoons tequila
7   tablespoons triple sec
⅓   cup fresh lime juice
2   tablespoons sugar
    Pinch of salt
4   small thin watermelon wedges

Puree first 7 ingredients in blender until smooth. Pour into chilled Margarita glasses. Garnish with watermelon wedges.

4 SERVINGS

Freezing the watermelon and strawberries before mixing the drink eliminates the need for ice—and allows the different fruit flavors to retain their full intensity.

◆ ◆ ◆

·MAIN COURSES·

Rib-Eye Steaks with Mushrooms, Brandy and Blue Cheese

◆ ◆ ◆

2   10- to 12-ounce rib-eye steaks (each about 1 inch thick)
1   tablespoon olive oil

3   tablespoons unsalted butter
1   small onion, thinly sliced
½   pound mushrooms, thickly sliced
4   garlic cloves, chopped
¾   cup canned beef broth
¼   cup brandy
¼   teaspoon minced fresh rosemary
1¼ cups crumbled blue cheese (about 4 ounces)

Fresh rosemary sprigs

Press the steaks to test for done-ness. Well-done feels firm and rare feels soft, while medium-rare feels springy to the touch, yielding with a little resistance.

Place steaks in shallow baking dish. Drizzle with olive oil; rub oil all over steaks. Sprinkle steaks with salt and pepper. Let steaks stand at room temperature for 1 hour.

Melt butter in heavy medium skillet over medium-high heat. Add onion and sauté until beginning to soften, about 3 minutes. Add mushrooms and garlic; sauté until mushrooms are just tender, about 4 minutes. Set mushroom mixture aside.

Heat heavy large skillet over medium-high heat. Add steaks to skillet; fry until cooked to desired doneness, about 5 minutes per side for medium-rare. Using tongs, transfer steaks to plates; tent loosely with aluminum foil to keep warm.

Add the broth, brandy and rose-mary to the skillet used to cook the steaks. Stir the mixture, scraping all the flavorful browned bits in the pan into the sauce. This is called deglazing.

Add broth, then brandy and minced rosemary to same large skillet and bring to boil, scraping up browned bits. Add mushroom mixture. Boil until liquid is thick enough to coat spoon lightly, about 5 minutes. Add 1 cup cheese; stir just until cheese melts, about 1 minute. Season sauce to taste with salt and pepper.

Spoon sauce over steaks. Sprinkle with remaining ¼ cup cheese. Garnish with rosemary sprigs.

2 SERVINGS

Meat and Mushroom Pies

♦ ♦ ♦

These savory pies filled with ground beef and mushrooms are a snap to make using purchased sheets of puff pastry for the crust. In fact, the whole dish comes together in less than 30 minutes, including baking.

1	frozen puff pastry sheet (half of 17¼-ounce package), thawed
10	ounces lean ground beef
¼	pound mushrooms, sliced
1	cup chopped onion
1¾	teaspoons dried thyme
1½	tablespoons all purpose flour
1	cup canned beef broth
1½	tablespoons steak sauce

Preheat oven to 450°F. Roll out pastry on floured surface to 10-inch square; cut in half diagonally. Using small plate as guide, cut out one 5½-inch-diameter pastry round from each half.

Heat heavy large skillet over medium-high heat. Add beef, mushrooms, onion and thyme. Sauté until beef is no longer pink, about 5 minutes. Add flour; stir 1 minute. Add broth and steak sauce; bring to boil. Reduce heat; simmer until sauce is thick, stirring often, about 5 minutes. Season with salt and pepper. Spoon beef into two 1¼-cup custard cups. Top with pastry rounds; press overhangs firmly to sides of cups. Cut 3 vents in each pastry round.

Bake pies until pastry is golden brown, about 12 minutes.

2 SERVINGS

Beef with Marrow Sauce and Glazed Onions

♦ ♦ ♦

3	pounds 1½-inch pieces beef marrow bones
3	cups beef stock or canned beef broth
1½	cups dry red wine
¾	cup ruby Port
6	8-ounce filet mignon steaks
1	tablespoon olive oil

3	tablespoons unsalted butter
18	ounces fresh wild mushrooms, sliced
3	large shallots, thinly sliced
1½	tablespoons minced garlic
3	plum tomatoes, seeded, diced
2	teaspoons chopped fresh parsley
	Glazed Onions (see recipe below)

Place marrow bones in large bowl. Cover with ice water. Chill overnight. Drain. Using small knife, push marrow out through bones. Coarsely crumble enough marrow to equal 1¼ cups.

Boil stock, wine and Port in heavy large saucepan until liquid is reduced to 1¼ cups, about 30 minutes.

Preheat oven to 450°F. Sprinkle steaks with salt and pepper. Heat 1 tablespoon oil in heavy large skillet over medium-high heat. Cook steaks in skillet until brown, about 2 minutes per side. Transfer steaks to rimmed baking sheet. Cook in oven to desired doneness, about 8 minutes for medium-rare. Keep warm.

Meanwhile, discard excess oil in skillet. Whisk stock mixture into skillet. Bring to boil, scraping up any browned bits. Strain into small saucepan; discard solids. Add 1¼ cups crumbled marrow; stir until melted. Keep sauce warm.

Melt butter in another large skillet over medium-high heat. Add mushrooms, shallots and garlic; sauté until mushrooms are golden, about 10 minutes. Stir in tomatoes and parsley. Season with salt and pepper. Serve steaks with sauce, mushroom mixture and onions.

6 SERVINGS

Your butcher should have the marrow bones for this rich and flavorful dish. Since the bones need to be refrigerated overnight, you'll want to start this recipe a day ahead.

Glazed Onions

3	tablespoons butter
30	pearl onions, blanched in boiling water 2 minutes, drained, peeled
⅓	cup water

Preheat oven to 450°F. Melt butter in large ovenproof skillet over medium heat. Add onions and sauté until golden, about 12 minutes. Stir in water. Transfer skillet to oven and cook until onions are tender and glazed, stirring occasionally, about 10 minutes.

6 SERVINGS

Beef Stew with Vegetables

◆ ◆ ◆

8	ounces bacon slices, coarsely chopped
8	tablespoons olive oil
6	pounds trimmed boneless beef chuck, cut into 1½-inch pieces
4	leeks (white and pale green parts only), coarsely chopped
6	tablespoons all purpose flour
3	14½-ounce cans diced tomatoes in juice
1	750-ml bottle dry red wine
3	cups canned beef broth
3	bay leaves
2	tablespoons chopped fresh thyme
1	tablespoon paprika (preferably Hungarian sweet)
2	pounds rutabagas, peeled, cut into 1-inch pieces
4	large carrots, peeled, cut into 1-inch pieces
4	zucchini, cut into 1-inch pieces
2	red bell peppers, cut into 1-inch pieces
1	tablespoon butter, room temperature

◆ ◆ ◆

This hearty stew is chock-full of good-for-you vegetables—rutabagas, carrots, zucchini and red bell peppers. It's an ideal choice for feeding a crowd since most of the cooking can be done up to a day ahead.

◆ ◆ ◆

Cook bacon in heavy large pot over medium-high heat until brown and crisp, about 8 minutes. Using slotted spoon, transfer bacon to small bowl. Add 6 tablespoons oil to drippings in pot. Increase heat to high. Sprinkle beef with salt and pepper. Working in batches, add beef to pot and sauté until no longer pink, about 4 minutes per batch. Using slotted spoon, transfer beef to large bowl.

Add remaining 2 tablespoons oil to pot. Add leeks and sauté until beginning to brown, scraping bottom of pan occasionally, about 8 minutes. Add 5 tablespoons flour and stir 1 minute. Return beef and any accumulated juices to pot. Mix in bacon, tomatoes with juices, wine, broth, bay leaves, thyme and paprika. Bring to boil. Reduce heat to medium-low. Cover pot and simmer 15 minutes. Add rutabagas and carrots. Cover and simmer 45 minutes. Uncover and simmer until meat is tender, stirring occasionally, about 30 minutes. *(Can be made 1 day ahead. Refrigerate. Bring to simmer.)*

Add zucchini and bell peppers to stew and simmer uncovered until zucchini and bell peppers are tender, stirring occasionally, about 7 minutes. Season stew to taste with salt and pepper. Mix butter and remaining 1 tablespoon flour in small bowl to blend; mix into stew. Simmer until sauce thickens, about 5 minutes.

18 SERVINGS

Grilled Skirt Steak with Cumin and Cilantro

◆ ◆ ◆

½   cup cumin seeds (about 1¾ ounces)
1   cup olive oil
½   cup fresh lime juice
6   tablespoons coarsely chopped seeded jalapeño chilies
    (about 4 large)
5   large garlic cloves, peeled
2   tablespoons cracked black pepper
2   large bunches cilantro with stems (about 6 ounces)

3   pounds skirt steak, excess fat trimmed, cut into 6 pieces total

Sauté cumin seeds in heavy medium skillet over medium-low heat until lightly toasted, about 6 minutes. Transfer seeds to blender. Add ¼ cup oil, lime juice, chilies, garlic and 2 tablespoons black pepper to blender. Blend until cumin is finely ground. Add cilantro and ¾ cup oil. Puree until smooth. Season with salt.

Transfer marinade to glass baking dish. Add steaks; turn to coat. Cover and chill, turning occasionally, 6 hours up to 1 day.

Prepare barbecue (medium-high heat). Remove steaks from marinade. Grill steaks to desired doneness, about 4 minutes per side for medium-rare. Cut steaks diagonally across grain and serve.

6 SERVINGS

Grilled Burgers with Roquefort Mayonnaise and Barbecued Red Onions

◆ ◆ ◆

8 ½-inch-thick slices red onions

1⅓ cups bottled hickory-flavored barbecue sauce

3 pounds ground round beef, formed into eight 4- to 5-inch diameter patties

8 4- to 5-inch-diameter hamburger buns, split
   Roquefort Mayonnaise (see recipe below)

Prepare barbecue (medium heat). Brush onions generously with barbecue sauce. Grill until onions are tender, brown and glazed, basting with barbecue sauce and turning occasionally, about 15 minutes.

Sprinkle patties with salt and pepper. Grill patties until cooked through, about 5 minutes per side. Grill hamburger buns, cut side down, until lightly toasted, about 2 minutes. Place patties on bottom halves of buns. Top each with 1 onion slice, Roquefort Mayonnaise, then bun tops. Serve immediately.

8 SERVINGS

Roquefort Mayonnaise

8 ounces Roquefort cheese, crumbled

⅔ cup mayonnaise

2 teaspoons red wine vinegar

1 teaspoon hot pepper sauce

Stir all ingredients in bowl to blend. *(Can be made 1 day ahead. Cover; chill. Bring to room temperature before using.)*

MAKES ABOUT 1½ CUPS

◆ ◆ ◆

BACK-YARD BARBECUE FOR EIGHT

GRILLED CLAMS WITH BASIL-BACON SALSA
(PAGE 13; PICTURED OPPOSITE)

GRILLED BURGERS WITH ROQUEFORT MAYONNAISE AND BARBECUED RED ONIONS
(AT LEFT; PICTURED OPPOSITE)

MIXED GREEN SALAD

CREAMY SUCCOTASH SALAD
(PAGE 156; PICTURED OPPOSITE)

BEER, LEMONADE AND ICED TEA

PEACH PIE À LA MODE

◆ ◆ ◆

Veal with Whipped Parsnips and Mushroom Cream Sauce

◆ ◆ ◆

2   tablespoons (¼ stick) butter
8   ounces assorted fresh wild mushrooms (such as crimini, oyster and stemmed shiitake), sliced
2   cups chicken stock or canned low-salt chicken broth
½   cup whipping cream
1   tablespoon finely chopped fresh parsley
1   teaspoon whole grain Dijon mustard

4   8-ounce veal rib chops (each 1¼ inches thick), boned

Whipped Parsnips (see recipe below)

Melt 1 tablespoon butter in heavy large skillet over medium-high heat. Add mushrooms and sauté until tender, about 8 minutes. Add chicken stock. Boil until mixture is reduced to 1½ cups, about 12 minutes. Stir in whipping cream, parsley and mustard. Season mushroom sauce with salt and pepper.

Meanwhile, sprinkle veal chops with salt and pepper. Melt remaining 1 tablespoon butter in another heavy large skillet over medium-high heat. Add veal and cook to desired doneness, about 4 minutes per side for medium-rare.

Spoon Whipped Parsnips onto 4 plates. Place veal chops atop parsnips. Spoon sauce around parsnips and serve.

4 SERVINGS

Whipped Parsnips

1   pound parsnips, peeled, cut into ½-inch pieces
1½ cups (about) whole milk
⅓   cup whipping cream

Combine parsnips, ¾ cup milk and whipping cream in heavy large saucepan. Cover and simmer over medium-low heat until parsnips are tender and most of liquid has evaporated, about 30 minutes. Transfer mixture to blender. Puree until smooth, thinning with more milk if necessary. Transfer to bowl. Season parsnips to taste with salt and pepper and serve.

4 SERVINGS

Veal and Mushroom Sauce over Polenta Squares

This rich tomato sauce, made with ground veal, mushrooms, rosemary and garlic, is also delicious served over a tubular pasta such as rigatoni.

◆ ◆ ◆

3   tablespoons olive oil
1   pound ground veal
3   large garlic cloves, chopped
1   tablespoon chopped fresh rosemary or 2 teaspoons dried
½   pound mushrooms, chopped
1   14½-ounce can diced tomatoes in puree
¾   cup dry red wine
¾   cup canned beef broth
¼   cup tomato paste
    Parmesan Polenta Squares (see recipe below)

Heat oil in large skillet over medium-high heat. Add veal, garlic and rosemary; sauté until veal is no longer pink, breaking up large clumps with back of spoon, about 5 minutes. Add mushrooms; sauté 5 minutes. Add tomatoes, wine, broth and tomato paste. Bring to boil. Reduce heat to medium; simmer until mixture thickens, stirring occasionally, about 30 minutes. Serve over polenta squares.

4 SERVINGS

Parmesan Polenta Squares

6   tablespoons yellow cornmeal
6   tablespoons white cornmeal
3   cups canned low-salt chicken broth
1   cup grated Parmesan cheese
    Olive oil

Whisk both cornmeals in bowl to blend. Bring broth to boil in heavy medium saucepan over medium-high heat. Gradually whisk in cornmeal. Reduce heat to medium-low; whisk constantly until mixture boils and becomes very thick, about 5 minutes. Remove from heat. Whisk in ½ cup Parmesan; season with salt and pepper. Pour polenta into 8 x 8 x 2-inch baking pan; smooth top. Cool until firm, at least 30 minutes, or cover and chill overnight.

Preheat broiler. Cut polenta into 16 squares; brush with oil. Arrange, oiled side down, on baking sheet. Brush top with oil. Broil until golden brown, 3 minutes per side. Sprinkle with Parmesan.

MAKES 16

Stuffed Veal Breast with Spinach

◆ ◆ ◆

1	pound ground veal
2	cups fresh breadcrumbs made from crustless French bread
1	10-ounce package frozen chopped spinach, thawed, squeezed dry
1	cup drained oil-packed sun-dried tomatoes, chopped
2	large eggs
3	tablespoons chopped fresh marjoram
2½	tablespoons minced garlic
1½	teaspoons salt
½	teaspoon black pepper
½	teaspoon ground nutmeg
1	3½- to 3¾-pound piece boneless veal breast, butterflied, pounded to 15 x 13-inch rectangle
2	tablespoons olive oil
6	cups coarsely chopped onions
3	cups coarsely chopped carrots
2	cups coarsely chopped celery
1	750-ml bottle dry red wine
3½	cups (about) chicken stock or canned low-salt chicken broth
1	14½- to 16-ounce can diced tomatoes in juice

Mix first 5 ingredients, 1 tablespoon marjoram, 1 tablespoon garlic, salt, pepper and nutmeg in large bowl to blend.

Preheat oven to 400°F. Place veal breast, pounded side up, on work surface. Sprinkle with salt and pepper. Form ground veal mixture into 8-inch-long, 3½-inch-wide loaf. Place loaf atop breast about 3 inches from 1 long side. Fold short sides of breast over. Fold long side nearest stuffing over. Roll up, enclosing stuffing. Tie in several places with twine. Fasten each short end with toothpicks.

Sprinkle veal with salt and pepper. Heat 1 tablespoon oil in heavy large skillet over high heat. Add veal; sauté until brown on all sides, about 10 minutes. Transfer to large roasting pan. Add 1 tablespoon oil, onions, carrots and celery to skillet; sauté until golden, about 15 minutes. Transfer to pan with veal. Add wine, 2 cups stock, tomatoes and remaining marjoram and garlic.

Roast veal until very tender, turning and basting with pan juices every 30 minutes and adding stock as needed to keep juices halfway up sides of veal, about 2 hours 30 minutes. Remove from oven. Transfer to platter; let stand 30 minutes. Remove twine. Slice veal. Transfer pan juices and vegetables to saucepan; rewarm. Season with salt and pepper. Spoon juices and vegetables around veal.

6 SERVINGS

Have your butcher order the veal breast, then ask him to bone, butterfly, and pound it, forming a rectangle that has the dimensions described in the recipe ingredients list.

◆ ◆ ◆

Braised Lamb Shanks with Fennel, Tomatoes, Turnips and Carrots

◆ ◆ ◆

First, heat the oil in a heavy large skillet over high heat until hot. Working in batches, add lamb shanks and brown well, turning with tongs.

Transfer marinade to same skillet and bring to boil, scraping up any browned bits. Pour marinade over shanks and vegetables in roasting pan (the marinade provides the liquid needed for oven braising). Next, cover the meat and vegetables before placing in the oven to bake.

TOPPING

½	cup chopped fresh parsley
1	tablespoon grated lemon peel
1	tablespoon grated orange peel
1	tablespoon minced garlic
1	teaspoon drained green peppercorns in brine, coarsely chopped

LAMB

1	14½-ounce can low-salt chicken broth
1	14½-ounce can beef broth
½	cup plus ⅓ cup dry red wine
⅔	cup red currant jelly
2	teaspoons herbes de Provence*
2	teaspoons red wine vinegar
3	garlic cloves, minced
6	lamb shanks (each about 1 pound)
3	tablespoons olive oil
1	pound plum tomatoes, each cut into 4 wedges, seeded
2	large turnips, peeled, cut into ¾-inch-thick wedges
2	large fennel bulbs, each cut into 4 wedges
3	large carrots, peeled, cut diagonally into ¾-inch-thick slices
1	cup chopped leek (white and pale green parts only)
¼	cup (½ stick) butter
⅓	cup all purpose flour
1	tablespoon tomato paste

FOR TOPPING: Mix all ingredients in medium bowl to blend. *(Can be prepared 8 hours ahead. Cover and refrigerate.)*

FOR LAMB: Whisk chicken broth, beef broth, ½ cup wine, ⅓ cup currant jelly, herbes de Provence, vinegar and garlic in large glass baking dish to blend. Add lamb shanks; turn to coat. Cover and chill overnight, turning occasionally.

Preheat oven to 325°F. Remove lamb from marinade; reserve marinade. Pat lamb dry with paper towels. Sprinkle with salt and

♦ ♦ ♦

RUSTIC SUPPER
FOR SIX

YELLOW BELL PEPPER SOUP
(PAGE 28)

BRAISED LAMB SHANKS WITH
FENNEL, TOMATOES, TURNIPS
AND CARROTS
(AT LEFT; PICTURED AT LEFT)

ROSEMARY MASHED POTATOES
(PAGE 142; PICTURED AT LEFT)

MERLOT

CHEESECAKE

♦ ♦ ♦

pepper. Heat oil in heavy large skillet over high heat. Working in batches, add lamb; cook until brown on all sides, about 8 minutes. Transfer to large roasting pan. Add all vegetables to roasting pan.

Pour reserved marinade into same skillet. Bring to boil, scraping up any browned bits. Pour over lamb. Cover; bake until lamb and vegetables are very tender, turning occasionally, about 2 hours. Using slotted spoon, transfer lamb and vegetables to large serving bowl. Tent with aluminum foil.

Spoon fat off top of cooking liquid. Melt butter in heavy large saucepan over medium-high heat. Add flour. Stir until golden, about 5 minutes. Whisk in cooking liquid. Add ⅓ cup wine, ⅓ cup jelly and tomato paste. Boil until sauce thickens enough to coat spoon, whisking occasionally, about 10 minutes. Season with salt and pepper. Spoon sauce, then topping, over lamb and vegetables.

A dried herb mixture available at specialty foods stores and some supermarkets. A combination of dried thyme, basil, savory and fennel seeds can be substituted.

6 SERVINGS

Lamb Brochettes with Cucumber and Tomato Tzatziki

◆ ◆ ◆

3½ pounds boneless leg of lamb, fat and sinew trimmed
6 tablespoons olive oil (preferably extra-virgin)
3 tablespoons fresh lemon juice
½ large onion, grated
2 large garlic cloves, minced
1 teaspoon dried oregano
1 teaspoon dried thyme

6 10- to 12-inch-long metal skewers
Cucumber and Tomato Tzatziki (see recipe below)

Cut trimmed lamb into 1¼- to 1½-inch cubes. Mix lamb and next 6 ingredients in glass baking dish. Cover mixture and refrigerate at least 4 hours and up to 8 hours, turning lamb occasionally.

Preheat broiler or prepare barbecue (medium-high heat). Divide lamb cubes among skewers. Sprinkle with salt and pepper. Arrange skewers on broiler pan or grill. Drizzle with any remaining marinade. Broil or grill lamb to desired doneness, turning occasionally, about 9 minutes for medium-rare. Serve hot with tzatziki.

6 SERVINGS

Cucumber and Tomato Tzatziki

3 cups plain yogurt (do not use low-fat or nonfat)
1 English hothouse cucumber, peeled, halved lengthwise, seeded
3 tablespoons finely chopped fresh dill
1 large garlic clove, minced
1 large tomato, quartered, seeded, thinly sliced

Place strainer over large bowl. Line strainer with 3 layers of cheesecloth. Spoon yogurt into lined strainer; let stand at room temperature to drain 3 hours (liquid will drain out and yogurt will thicken). Transfer yogurt to medium bowl; discard liquid.

Meanwhile, coarsely grate cucumber. Place in another strainer; let stand at room temperature until most of liquid drains out, about 3 hours. Discard liquid. Squeeze excess moisture from cucumber.

Mix grated cucumber, dill and garlic into yogurt. *(Can be made 1 day ahead. Cover and chill.)* Mix tomato into yogurt.

6 SERVINGS

Spicy Lamb with Tomato and Cilantro

◆ ◆ ◆

1	tablespoon olive oil
1	large onion, chopped
3	large garlic cloves, chopped
3	jalapeño chilies, seeded, chopped
2½	teaspoons ground cumin
1	pound lamb stew meat, cut into scant ½-inch pieces
1½	cups tomato sauce
⅓	cup canned beef broth
¼	cup chopped fresh cilantro

Heat oil in large skillet over medium-high heat. Add onion, garlic, chilies and cumin and sauté until onion begins to soften, about 3 minutes. Sprinkle lamb with salt and pepper. Add to skillet and sauté until no longer pink, about 5 minutes. Add tomato sauce and broth. Bring to boil. Cover skillet, reduce heat to medium-low and simmer until lamb is tender, about 45 minutes. Season to taste with salt and pepper. Sprinkle with cilantro and serve.

4 SERVINGS

◆ ◆ ◆

Here's a hearty lamb dish with just the right amount of spice, thanks to three jalapeño chilies. It comes together in an hour and it's perfect with mashed potatoes.

◆ ◆ ◆

Rack of Lamb with Port and Black Olive Sauce

◆ ◆ ◆

2	cups beef stock or canned beef broth
2	cups chicken stock or canned low-salt chicken broth
⅔	cup ruby Port
⅓	cup minced shallots
2	teaspoons minced fresh thyme
2	tablespoons (¼ stick) unsalted butter, room temperature
1	tablespoon all purpose flour
2	1¼- to 1½-pound racks of lamb, trimmed
¼	cup Dijon mustard
¾	cup (packed) fresh breadcrumbs from crustless French bread
¾	cup freshly grated Parmesan cheese (about 2¼ ounces)
6	tablespoons chopped fresh parsley
3	tablespoons unsalted butter, melted

1½ tablespoons minced garlic

½ cup chopped pitted Kalamata olives or
    other brine-cured black olives

Boil first 5 ingredients in heavy large saucepan over medium-high heat until mixture is reduced to 1½ cups, about 35 minutes. Mix 2 tablespoons butter and flour in small bowl to form paste. Whisk paste into sauce; simmer until slightly thickened, about 3 minutes. Strain into heavy small saucepan.

Preheat oven to 450°F. Place lamb on baking sheet. Spread mustard over lamb. Mix breadcrumbs, cheese, parsley, butter and garlic in small bowl; press onto lamb. Bake lamb to desired doneness, about 25 minutes for medium-rare.

Bring sauce to simmer. Mix in chopped olives. Cut lamb between ribs into chops. Serve lamb with sauce.

4 SERVINGS

◆ ◆ ◆

ELEGANT FIRESIDE DINNER FOR FOUR

RED CAVIAR DIP
(PAGE 22)

RACK OF LAMB WITH PORT AND
BLACK OLIVE SAUCE
(AT LEFT; PICTURED AT LEFT)

SAUTÉED SPINACH

BABY CARROTS

MERLOT

LEMON TART WITH
FROZEN LIME CREAM
(PAGE 178)

◆ ◆ ◆

Grilled Lamb Chops with Red Wine, Garlic and Honey Glaze

◆ ◆ ◆

¾	cup dry red wine
¼	cup olive oil
3	tablespoons chopped fresh oregano
2	tablespoons minced garlic
2	teaspoons red wine vinegar
½	teaspoon salt
½	teaspoon black pepper
8	1- to 1¼-inch-thick loin lamb chops, fat well trimmed
2	tablespoons honey

Mix first 7 ingredients in large glass baking dish. Arrange lamb chops in single layer in dish; turn to coat with marinade. Cover and refrigerate at least 2 hours, turning and basting often. *(Can be prepared 1 day ahead. Keep refrigerated.)*

Prepare barbecue (medium-high heat). Transfer lamb to plate. Mix honey into marinade. Grill lamb to desired doneness, turning and basting with marinade often, about 10 minutes for medium-rare.

4 SERVINGS

Moroccan-Style Lamb Chops

◆ ◆ ◆

2	½-inch-thick slices crustless French bread (each about 3 x 5 inches)
2	teaspoons minced garlic
2	teaspoons grated orange peel
1	teaspoon ground cumin
¼	teaspoon cayenne pepper
1½	teaspoons olive oil
6	¾-inch-thick lamb rib chops

Preheat oven to 500°F. Grind bread in processor to fine crumbs. Add garlic, peel, cumin and cayenne. Drizzle in olive oil and blend until crumbs are evenly moistened. Transfer mixture to plate. Sprinkle chops with salt. Dip both sides of chops into mixture, pressing crumbs onto lamb. Arrange chops on baking sheet.

Bake lamb chops until crumb coating is golden and lamb is cooked to desired doneness, 12 minutes for medium-rare.

2 SERVINGS

◆ ◆ ◆

GREEK-STYLE DINNER FOR FOUR

LEMONY WHITE BEAN SKORDALIA WITH GRILL-TOASTED PITA
(PAGE 25; PICTURED OPPOSITE)

GRILLED LAMB CHOPS WITH RED WINE, GARLIC AND HONEY GLAZE
(AT LEFT; PICTURED OPPOSITE)

CHOPPED VEGETABLE SALAD WITH FETA AND OLIVES
(PAGE 148; PICTURED OPPOSITE)

RETSINA OR SAUVIGNON BLANC

COFFEE ICE CREAM AND BAKLAVA

◆ ◆ ◆

Roasted Spiced Pork Loin
with Root Vegetables

◆ ◆ ◆

Using a mortar and pestle or a coffee grinder, finely grind the cumin seeds, salt, peppercorns and cardamom seeds. Rub olive oil, then the spice mixture over the pork; let set 4 to 24 hours before roasting.

To check for proper doneness, insert an instant-read thermometer straight down from the top center of the pork roast; look for an internal temperature reading of 150°F.

SAUCE

6	bacon slices, cut in half
6	cups canned low-salt chicken broth
1½	cups dry white wine
½	cup red currant jelly
1¼	teaspoons minced fresh rosemary
3	tablespoons unsalted butter

PORK

2	teaspoons cumin seeds
2	teaspoons coarse salt
1	teaspoon black peppercorns
1	teaspoon black cardamom seeds (from about 30 whole green or white cardamom pods)
1	4- to 4¼-pound center-cut boneless pork loin (about 10 inches long and 3½ inches in diameter)
1	tablespoon olive oil
2½	pounds large russet potatoes (about 5), peeled, halved lengthwise, cut into 2-inch pieces
1½	pounds large parsnips (about 4), peeled, cut into 2-inch pieces, thick portions halved lengthwise
1½	pounds large carrots (about 4), peeled, cut into 2-inch pieces, thick portions halved lengthwise
8	large shallots, peeled, halved
8	large garlic cloves, peeled
3	large fresh rosemary sprigs
6	tablespoons olive oil
8	medium beets, peeled, cut into 1-inch wedges

FOR SAUCE: Cook bacon in heavy large saucepan over medium heat until crisp. Using tongs, transfer bacon to paper towels. Discard drippings from pan. Add broth, wine, jelly and rosemary to pan. Boil until reduced to 2½ cups, about 35 minutes. Return bacon to sauce. Boil until liquid is reduced to 1⅓ cups, about 10 minutes longer. Strain sauce into small saucepan. Add butter. Whisk over low heat until sauce is smooth, about 2 minutes. Season with salt and pepper. *(Can be prepared 1 day ahead. Cover and refrigerate.)*

FOR PORK: Finely grind first 4 ingredients. Place pork loin in 13 x 9 x 2-inch glass baking dish. Rub oil, then spice mixture all over pork. Cover; refrigerate 4 hours and up to 1 day.

Position racks in center and bottom third of oven and preheat to 400°F. Place potatoes, parsnips, carrots, halved shallots, garlic cloves and rosemary sprigs in large roasting pan. Drizzle with 5 tablespoons oil; sprinkle with salt and pepper. Roast on center rack for 45 minutes, turning vegetables occasionally.

Place beets in small roasting pan. Drizzle with 1 tablespoon oil; sprinkle with salt and pepper. Remove large roasting pan from oven. Push vegetables to sides of pan, clearing space in center for pork. Place pork in center of pan. Return large roasting pan to center rack. Place pan with beets on bottom rack.

Roast pork with vegetables until vegetables are brown and cooked through and thermometer inserted into center of pork registers 150°F, turning vegetables occasionally, about 1 hour. Roast beets until tender, turning occasionally, about 1 hour. Remove pork and all vegetables from oven and let stand 10 minutes.

Place pork roast in center of large platter; surround with all vegetables. Rewarm sauce over low heat, whisking constantly. Transfer sauce to gravy dish. Serve pork and vegetables with sauce.

8 SERVINGS

♦ ♦ ♦

DINNER WITH CO-WORKERS FOR EIGHT

ORANGE-MARINATED OLIVES
(PAGE 24)

MIXED GREEN SALAD

ROASTED SPICED PORK LOIN WITH ROOT VEGETABLES
(AT LEFT; PICTURED AT LEFT)

STEAMED BROCCOLI

SYRAH

BREAD AND BUTTER PUDDING
(PAGE 203)

♦ ♦ ♦

Medallions of Pork with Dried Cherry Sauce

◆ ◆ ◆

4   8-ounce pork loin chops with bone, trimmed (1 inch thick)
2   tablespoons olive oil
2½ cups canned low-salt chicken broth
⅓   cup dried cherries (about 2 ounces)
⅓   cup balsamic vinegar

Using sharp knife, cut bones from pork chops. Cover and refrigerate pork. Heat 1 tablespoon oil in heavy medium skillet over medium-high heat. Add bones; sauté until brown, about 15 minutes. Pour off any accumulated fat. Add 2 cups broth to skillet. Simmer over low heat until broth is reduced to 1 cup, scraping up any browned bits, about 25 minutes. Remove bones. Add cherries and vinegar to skillet; simmer until reduced to ⅔ cup, about 8 minutes. *(Can be made 1 day ahead. Cover and chill.)*

Sprinkle pork with salt and pepper. Heat 1 tablespoon oil in heavy large skillet over medium-high heat. Add pork; sauté until brown, about 2 minutes per side. Add remaining ½ cup chicken broth. Reduce heat to low. Cover and cook until pork is just firm and no longer pink in center, about 6 minutes. Transfer pork to plates. Tent pork with foil to keep warm.

Pour cherry mixture into same skillet. Bring to boil. Reduce heat; simmer until sauce is reduced to ¾ cup and coats back of spoon, about 5 minutes. Season with salt and pepper. Spoon over pork.

4 SERVINGS

◆ ◆ ◆

SATURDAY NIGHT DINNER FOR FOUR

Escarole Salad with Shiitake Mushrooms and Pancetta
(PAGE 154)

Medallions of Pork with Dried Cherry Sauce
(AT RIGHT; PICTURED AT RIGHT)

Butternut Squash and Sage Orzo
(PAGE 141; PICTURED AT RIGHT)

Beaujolais

Gingerbread with Vanilla Ice Cream

◆ ◆ ◆

Ham and Spring Vegetable Salad with Shallot Vinaigrette

◆ ◆ ◆

1½   pounds small red-skinned potatoes, each cut into 8 wedges

1½   pounds baby carrots, peeled, cut lengthwise in half

1½   pounds asparagus, trimmed, cut into 2-inch pieces

6   ounces sugar snap peas, trimmed

18   ounces low-fat smoked ham, cut into ¼-inch-thick slices, then into 2-inch-long by ½-inch-wide pieces
    Shallot Vinaigrette (see recipe below)

1   6-ounce package fresh baby spinach

Cook potatoes and carrots in large pot of boiling salted water until almost tender, about 7 minutes. Add asparagus and peas; cook until vegetables are just tender, about 3 minutes longer. Drain. Rinse with cold water; drain. Transfer to large bowl. *(Can be prepared 1 day ahead. Cover and refrigerate.)*

Add ham to vegetables. Add Shallot Vinaigrette to salad and toss to coat. Season to taste with salt and pepper.

Line bowl or platter with spinach. Top with salad and serve.

8 SERVINGS

Shallot Vinaigrette

½   cup chopped shallots

6   tablespoons seasoned rice vinegar*

1½   teaspoons Dijon mustard

1½   tablespoons olive oil

Whisk shallots, rice vinegar and Dijon mustard in small bowl to blend. Gradually whisk in oil. Season with salt and pepper.

Also known as sushi vinegar; available at Asian markets and in the Asian foods section of some supermarkets.

MAKES ABOUT ¾ CUP

Serve this delicious main-course salad with crisp flatbread, such as lavash. Because it can be eaten at cool room temperature, it's an ideal choice for a buffet or potluck party.

◆ ◆ ◆

Pork and Ham Loaf with Marmalade-Mustard Glaze

◆ ◆ ◆

¼	cup (½ stick) unsalted butter
1	cup finely chopped onion
¾	cup finely chopped green bell pepper
1½	pounds ground pork
1	pound finely chopped smoked ham (about 3½ cups)
1	cup finely crushed saltine crackers
1	cup milk
2	large eggs, beaten to blend
1	teaspoon black pepper
¾	teaspoon salt
½	cup orange marmalade
½	cup Dijon mustard
⅓	cup (packed) golden brown sugar

Preheat oven to 350°F. Melt butter in heavy medium skillet over medium-low heat. Add onion and bell pepper. Cover and cook until vegetables are tender, stirring occasionally, about 10 minutes. Cool mixture completely.

Mix ground pork, ham, crushed crackers, milk, eggs, pepper, salt and cooled onion mixture in large bowl; combine thoroughly. Transfer pork mixture to shallow baking pan. Shape into 9 x 4 x 2½-inch loaf. Using long knife, make shallow crisscross (diamond) pattern in top of loaf. Bake loaf 30 minutes.

Meanwhile, blend orange marmalade, Dijon mustard and brown sugar in small bowl for glaze.

Drizzle ⅓ cup glaze over loaf; bake 15 minutes. Drizzle another ⅓ cup glaze over loaf; bake 15 minutes. Drizzle remaining glaze over loaf and bake until thermometer inserted into center of loaf registers 165°F, about 20 minutes longer. Transfer loaf to platter; let stand 10 minutes. Pour pan juices into small bowl; whisk to blend.

Cut loaf crosswise into ¾-inch-thick slices. Serve with pan juices.

6 TO 8 SERVINGS

◆ ◆ ◆

HOMESTYLE DINNER FOR SIX

ROMAINE SALAD WITH
THOUSAND ISLAND DRESSING
(PAGE 157)

PORK AND HAM LOAF WITH
MARMALADE-MUSTARD GLAZE
(AT LEFT; PICTURED OPPOSITE)

BUTTERED PEAS

MASHED POTATOES WITH CARROTS
(PAGE 145; PICTURED OPPOSITE)

CORN BREAD

BEER OR DRY RED WINE

WARM WALNUT BROWNIE PUDDING
(PAGE 204; PICTURED OPPOSITE)

◆ ◆ ◆

Mustard-braised Chicken

◆ ◆ ◆

3	tablespoons olive oil
2	tablespoons minced fresh thyme
3	teaspoons minced fresh marjoram
1½	teaspoons dry mustard
1	teaspoon minced fresh rosemary
1	3½-pound chicken, cut into 8 pieces
1½	cups finely chopped onion
2	tablespoons minced garlic
1	cup dry white wine
1	cup canned low-salt chicken broth
6	tablespoons Dijon mustard

Stir 1 tablespoon oil, 1 tablespoon thyme, 1½ teaspoons marjoram, dry mustard and ½ teaspoon rosemary in small bowl until paste forms. Rub paste all over chicken. Place in large bowl; refrigerate for 2 hours or overnight.

Heat 2 tablespoons oil in heavy large pot over medium-high heat. Sprinkle chicken with salt and pepper. Add chicken to pot and cook until brown on all sides, about 12 minutes. Transfer to bowl.

Add onion to pot; sauté over medium-high heat until tender, about 8 minutes. Add garlic; sauté 2 minutes. Add wine, broth, Dijon mustard and 1 tablespoon thyme, 1½ teaspoons marjoram and ½ teaspoon rosemary to pot. Bring to boil. Return chicken to pot. Reduce heat to medium-low. Cover and simmer until chicken is cooked through, approximately 25 minutes.

Transfer chicken to platter; cover to keep warm. Boil liquid in pot until thickened to sauce consistency, whisking often, 10 minutes. Season sauce with salt and pepper. Pour over chicken.

4 SERVINGS

◆ ◆ ◆

BISTRO DINNER FOR FOUR

TRIO OF SALADS
(PAGE 152; PICTURED OPPOSITE)

MUSTARD-BRAISED CHICKEN
(AT RIGHT; PICTURED OPPOSITE)

FRENCH FRIES

RED OR WHITE BURGUNDY

CHOCOLATE SOUFFLÉS WITH
WHITE CHOCOLATE CREAM
(PAGE 200)

◆ ◆ ◆

Chicken and Green Olive Enchiladas

◆ ◆ ◆

◆ ◆ ◆

8	tablespoons (about) olive oil
2	cups finely chopped onions
3	tablespoons chopped garlic
1	teaspoon dried oregano
1	teaspoon ground cumin
¼	teaspoon ground cinnamon
5	tablespoons hot Mexican-style chili powder
3	tablespoons all purpose flour
4½	cups canned low-salt chicken broth
½	ounce semisweet chocolate
16	5- to 6-inch corn tortillas
5	cups shredded cooked chicken
1	pound Monterey Jack cheese, coarsely grated (about 4½ cups)
1	cup drained pimiento-stuffed green olives, sliced

Heat 3 tablespoons oil in large saucepan over medium-low heat. Add 1 cup onion, garlic, oregano, cumin and cinnamon. Cover. Cook until onion is almost tender, stirring occasionally, about 10 minutes. Mix in chili powder and flour; stir 3 minutes. Gradually whisk in broth. Increase heat to medium-high. Boil until reduced to 3 cups, stirring occasionally, about 35 minutes. Remove from heat. Whisk in chocolate; season with salt and pepper. Cool.

Heat 1 tablespoon oil in medium skillet over medium heat. Add 1 tortilla and cook until just pliable, about 20 seconds per side. Transfer to paper-towel-lined baking sheet. Repeat with remaining tortillas, adding more oil as needed.

Spread ⅓ cup sauce in each of two 13 x 9 x 2-inch glass baking dishes. Mix 1 cup sauce with chicken in large bowl. Arrange 8 tortillas on work surface. Spoon 3 tablespoons cheese, 1 tablespoon olives, 1 tablespoon onion and ¼ cup chicken over center of each. Roll up tortillas. Arrange enchiladas seam side down in prepared dish. Repeat with remaining tortillas, 1½ cups cheese, olives, onion and chicken. *(Can be prepared 1 day ahead. Cover sauce and enchiladas separately; refrigerate.)*

Preheat oven to 375°F. Top enchiladas with remaining sauce, then sprinkle with remaining cheese. Cover with foil; bake 20 minutes (30 minutes if chilled). Remove foil and bake until sauce bubbles, about 10 minutes. Let stand 10 minutes.

8 SERVINGS

Green-Curry Chicken with Peas and Basil

◆ ◆ ◆

2   teaspoons olive oil
1   cup chopped onion
2   teaspoons minced fresh ginger
1   pound skinless boneless chicken breast halves, cut into strips
1   cup canned unsweetened coconut milk
½   cup canned low-salt chicken broth
1   tablespoon Thai green curry paste*
4   tablespoons thinly sliced fresh basil
1   tablespoon chopped fresh cilantro
1½ cups snow peas, stringed
¼   cup thinly sliced green onions
    Cooked rice

Heat oil in large skillet over medium-high heat. Add onion and 1 teaspoon ginger; sauté until fragrant, 1 minute. Add chicken; sauté until golden, 3 minutes. Using slotted spoon, transfer to bowl. Add coconut milk, broth and curry paste to skillet. Stir until smooth. Add 2 tablespoons basil, cilantro and 1 teaspoon ginger. Bring to boil. Reduce heat; simmer until sauce thickens, about 7 minutes. Return chicken mixture to skillet. Add snow peas and green onions; simmer until chicken is cooked, 5 minutes. Season with salt and pepper.

Spoon rice onto plates. Spoon curry atop rice. Sprinkle with remaining 2 tablespoons basil and serve.

*Thai green curry paste is available at Asian markets and in the Asian foods section of some supermarkets.

4 SERVINGS

◆ ◆ ◆

NEW ASIAN DINNER FOR FOUR

VIETNAMESE-STYLE SPRING ROLLS
WITH SHRIMP
(PAGE 18)

SOMEN WITH GINGER AND
FRESH VEGETABLES
(PAGE 139)

GREEN-CURRY CHICKEN WITH
PEAS AND BASIL
(AT LEFT; PICTURED AT LEFT)

THAI BEER

HOT OR ICED JASMINE TEA

MANGO SORBET WITH LYCHEES

◆ ◆ ◆

Roast Chicken with Tarragon

◆ ◆ ◆

Begin by roasting the chicken breast side down, which helps keep the breast meat moist and tender. After the chicken has roasted for 30 minutes, insert large kitchen fork into main cavity of chicken and turn chicken over, breast side up.

Roast chicken until meat thermometer inserted into innermost part of thigh registers 180°F. Make sure the thermometer is inserted deep enough for the sensor to register, and be careful not to hit the bone.

CHICKEN

2	teaspoons vegetable oil
1	7½-pound whole roasting chicken, excess fat from tail reserved, neck and heart cut into 1-inch pieces
1	cup chopped onion
1	cup chopped peeled carrots
4	cups cold water
2	large fresh parsley sprigs
1	fresh thyme sprig
6	whole black peppercorns
1	bay leaf

JUS

1	large shallot, minced
2	teaspoons chopped fresh tarragon
2	tablespoons (¼ stick) chilled unsalted butter, cut into pieces

FOR CHICKEN: Heat oil in heavy medium saucepan over medium heat. Add reserved chicken fat and sauté until fat is rendered and solid pieces are brown, about 8 minutes. Strain rendered fat into small bowl. Reserve solid fat pieces.

Freeze 2 tablespoons rendered chicken fat. Heat 1 tablespoon rendered fat in same saucepan over medium-high heat. Add neck and heart pieces and sauté until brown, about 8 minutes. Add ½ cup onion and ½ cup carrots; sauté until vegetables are tender, scraping up any browned bits, about 3 minutes. Add 4 cups cold water and reserved solid fat pieces. Bring to boil. Add parsley, thyme, peppercorns and bay leaf. Simmer over low heat until stock is reduced to 2 cups, about 2 hours 30 minutes. *(Stock can be prepared 1 day ahead. Cover and refrigerate.)*

Rinse chicken inside and out; pat dry with paper towels. Let stand at room temperature 30 minutes.

Preheat oven to 400°F. Rub 2 tablespoons frozen fat over chicken. Sprinkle chicken inside and out with salt and pepper. Place chicken, breast side down, on rack in heavy large roasting pan.

Fill main cavity with ½ cup onion and ½ cup carrots. Roast chicken until skin is pale golden and begins to crisp, about 30 minutes. Remove from oven. Insert large kitchen fork into main cavity of chicken and turn chicken breast side up. Roast until meat thermometer inserted into innermost part of thigh registers 180°F, about 1 hour 15 minutes longer. Transfer chicken to platter. Tent with aluminum foil while preparing jus.

FOR JUS: Pour pan juices into 4-cup glass measuring cup. Do not clean roasting pan. Strain chicken stock into pan juices, pressing on solids to release liquid. Freeze stock mixture 5 minutes.

Spoon fat off top of stock mixture and place 1 tablespoon fat in same roasting pan. Heat fat over medium heat. Add shallot and sauté until tender, about 2 minutes. Add stock mixture and tarragon and bring to boil, scraping up browned bits. Boil until reduced to 1 cup, about 8 minutes. Remove from heat. Add butter, 1 piece at a time, and whisk until melted and well blended. Season jus with salt and pepper. Serve chicken with jus.

4 SERVINGS

♦ ♦ ♦

SUNDAY FAMILY DINNER FOR FOUR

ROAST CHICKEN WITH TARRAGON
(AT LEFT; PICTURED AT LEFT)

ROASTED POTATOES, CARROTS AND
SHALLOTS WITH ROSEMARY
(PAGE 140; PICTURED AT LEFT)

SPINACH WITH
ROQUEFORT CHEESE
(PAGE 144)

PINOT NOIR

APPLE TART

♦ ♦ ♦

A ROOT REVOLUTION

Chances are, you can't name a person who doesn't like potatoes. But it's highly likely you could conjure up several who don't like the other root vegetables, namely rutabagas, parsnips, turnips, sweet potatoes and celery root. This is probably because their only experiences with these roots were way back when, back in the days of recipes that dictated root vegetables be overcooked and mashed beyond recognition. The new root vegetable dishes that are cropping up on restaurant menus, in cookbooks and in magazines are worth a re-try.

Today, with the current interest in reinterpreting old-fashioned foods in fresher-tasting and more healthful ways, we have what you could call a root revolution. Gone are the boiled-to-death roots of times past; now they are oven-roasted to subtle perfection, simmered in fragrant broth, stewed with interesting spices and highlighted in creamy purees. We've rediscovered their fresh, slightly sweet flavor, and also learned just how easy they are to prepare.

So the next time you're in the market, consider adding a couple of roots to your cart. Then reacquaint yourself with their flavorful possibilities.

◆ ◆ ◆

Moroccan-Style Chicken and Root Vegetable Stew

◆ ◆ ◆

1	tablespoon olive oil
12	ounces skinless boneless chicken breast halves, cut into 1-inch pieces
1½	cups chopped onion
2	garlic cloves, minced
1	tablespoon curry powder
1	tablespoon ground cumin
1	cinnamon stick
2	cups ½-inch pieces peeled red-skinned sweet potatoes (yams)
2	cups ½-inch pieces peeled parsnips
2	cups ½-inch pieces peeled turnips
1	cup ½-inch pieces peeled rutabaga
2	cups canned low-salt chicken broth
¼	cup dried currants or raisins
1	cup drained canned diced tomatoes
	Cooked couscous
	Chopped fresh cilantro

Heat oil in heavy large pot over medium-high heat. Sprinkle chicken with salt and pepper. Add chicken to pot and sauté until light golden but not cooked through, 1 minute. Transfer to bowl.

Add onion to pot and sauté until golden, about 4 minutes. Add garlic and stir 1 minute. Add curry powder, cumin and cinnamon stick and stir 30 seconds. Add sweet potatoes, parsnips, turnips, rutabaga, broth and currants. Cover and simmer until vegetables are tender, about 20 minutes. Add tomatoes and chicken with any accumulated juices to pot. Simmer until chicken is cooked through and flavors blend, about 5 minutes longer. Spoon stew over couscous. Sprinkle with chopped cilantro and serve.

6 SERVINGS

Herb-grilled Chicken Breasts, Thai Style

◆ ◆ ◆

⅓	cup finely chopped fresh basil
⅓	cup finely chopped fresh mint
⅓	cup finely chopped cilantro
3	tablespoons finely chopped peeled fresh ginger
4	garlic cloves
1½	tablespoons soy sauce
1½	tablespoons fish sauce (nam pla)*
1½	tablespoons canola oil
1½	tablespoons (packed) dark brown sugar
1	serrano chili, stemmed, chopped
6	skinless boneless chicken breast halves (about 2½ pounds total)

Combine first 10 ingredients in processor. Process until well blended, scraping down sides of bowl occasionally.

Arrange chicken in 13 x 9 x 2-inch glass dish. Spoon herb mixture over chicken, covering completely. Cover dish and chill at least 2 hours, turning chicken occasionally. *(Can be made 1 day ahead.)*

Meanwhile, prepare barbecue (medium-high heat). Grill chicken until cooked through, about 5 minutes per side.

Cut chicken crosswise into thin slices. Transfer to plates.

*Fish sauce (nam pla) is available at Asian markets.

6 SERVINGS

◆ ◆ ◆

LIGHT THAI MENU FOR SIX

SHRIMP BROTH WITH
LEMONGRASS, CHILI AND GINGER
(PAGE 30)

HERB-GRILLED CHICKEN BREASTS,
THAI STYLE
(AT LEFT; PICTURED AT LEFT)

SPICY SESAME NOODLE, GREEN
BEAN AND CARROT SALAD
(PAGE 158; PICTURED AT LEFT)

MINTED ICED TEA

PASSION FRUIT SORBET WITH
FRESH PINEAPPLE

◆ ◆ ◆

Pan-braised Chicken with Dried Fruits and Olives

◆ ◆ ◆

2   skinless boneless chicken breast halves
1   teaspoon ground cumin
2   tablespoons olive oil
2   garlic cloves, finely chopped
¾   cup mixed dried fruits (about 3 ounces), large pieces halved
½   cup dry white wine
½   cup canned low-salt chicken broth
8   brine-cured cracked green olives

Sprinkle chicken on all sides with cumin, salt and pepper. Heat oil in heavy medium skillet over medium heat. Add chicken and sauté until brown, about 2 minutes per side. Push chicken to side of skillet. Add garlic to skillet and stir 30 seconds. Add dried fruits, wine, broth and olives and bring to boil. Simmer chicken uncovered until just cooked through, turning chicken occasionally with tongs, about 10 minutes. Transfer chicken to plates. Increase heat and boil until sauce is slightly thickened, about 4 minutes. Spoon sauce over.

2 SERVINGS

◆ ◆ ◆

This recipe was inspired by the Chicken Marbella recipe in *The Silver Palate Cookbook*. It's especially good with couscous and baby carrots tossed with chopped fresh mint.

◆ ◆ ◆

Creamy Chicken-Noodle Casserole with Spinach and Mushrooms

◆ ◆ ◆

1   pound skinless boneless chicken breast halves
1½   cups (about) water
2   large garlic cloves, minced
1   bay leaf

⅓   cup all purpose flour
2   tablespoons cornstarch
2   cups low-fat milk
1   teaspoon dried tarragon
1   teaspoon salt
⅛   teaspoon ground nutmeg
¼   cup dry white wine
1   10-ounce package frozen spinach, thawed, squeezed dry

8   ounces spinach fettuccine

◆ ◆ ◆

Low-fat milk is the base for the cream sauce in this home-style main course. If spinach fettuccine is unavailable, the regular white variety will work every bit as well.

◆ ◆ ◆

8   ounces mushrooms, sliced
1½ teaspoons olive oil
¾   cup coarse fresh breadcrumbs from French bread
¼   cup freshly grated Parmesan cheese

Combine chicken, 1 cup water, garlic and bay leaf in large saucepan. Cover and simmer just until chicken is cooked through, turning once, about 15 minutes. Transfer chicken to plate; cool. Shred chicken. Pour cooking liquid into measuring cup, adding more water to measure 1 cup if necessary. Reserve cooking liquid.

Whisk flour and cornstarch in heavy large saucepan. Add 1 cup milk; whisk until smooth. Stir in 1 cup milk, tarragon, salt, nutmeg and reserved 1 cup chicken cooking liquid. Stir over medium heat until mixture thickens and boils, about 5 minutes. Add wine; stir until mixture is very thick, about 2 minutes longer. Remove from heat. Stir in shredded chicken and spinach. *(Can be made 1 day ahead. Cover; chill. Rewarm over medium-low heat, stirring frequently.)*

Preheat oven to 400°F. Oil 11 x 7 x 2-inch glass baking dish. Cook fettuccine in large pot of boiling salted water until just tender but still firm to bite. Drain. Return to pot. Add mushrooms and chicken; toss. Season with salt and pepper. Transfer to dish. Heat oil in small nonstick skillet over medium-high heat. Add breadcrumbs; stir 1 minute. Sprinkle over casserole. Bake until golden, 20 minutes. Let stand 10 minutes. Sprinkle with Parmesan.

6 SERVINGS

Tuscan-Style Peppered Chicken

◆ ◆ ◆

2   3½-pound chickens, halved, backbones removed
8   tablespoons olive oil (preferably extra-virgin)
2   tablespoons coarsely ground black pepper

Lemon wedges

Rub each chicken half all over with 2 tablespoons olive oil, then 1½ teaspoons pepper. Sprinkle generously with salt. Let chicken stand at room temperature for 1 hour.

Preheat broiler. Arrange chicken, skin side down, on broiler pan. Watching closely to avoid burning, broil chicken 5 to 6 inches from heat source until golden brown, about 12 minutes. Remove broiler pan from oven. Using tongs, transfer chicken to plate. Pour off any pan drippings. Return chicken, skin side up, to broiler pan. Broil until skin is crisp and golden brown, about 5 minutes. Turn chicken over, skin side down again, and broil until cooked through, 8 minutes. Transfer to platter; let stand 5 minutes. Serve with lemon.

4 SERVINGS

Chicken Thighs with
Creole Mustard-Orange Sauce

◆ ◆ ◆

4   small skinless boneless chicken thighs (about 12 ounces)
1½   tablespoons olive oil
¾   cup orange juice
¾   cup canned low-salt chicken broth
¼   cup Creole or whole-grain Dijon mustard
1   tablespoon honey
1   teaspoon hot pepper sauce

Sprinkle chicken on both sides with salt and pepper. Heat oil in heavy medium skillet over medium-high heat. Add chicken and sauté until brown, about 6 minutes per side. Add orange juice and broth to skillet. Simmer until chicken is cooked through, about 5 minutes. Transfer chicken to plate. Add mustard, honey and pepper sauce to skillet. Increase heat and boil until sauce thickens, about 7 minutes. Return chicken to skillet. Simmer until heated through, 1 minute. Transfer chicken to plates; top with sauce.

2 SERVINGS

Broiled Chicken with Thyme, Fennel and Peppers

◆ ◆ ◆

3   small fennel bulbs (about 2¾ pounds), trimmed, quartered lengthwise

3   red bell peppers, cut into 1-inch-wide strips
2   tablespoons olive oil (preferably extra-virgin)
3   teaspoons chopped fresh thyme

6   boneless chicken breasts

2   tablespoons (¼ stick) butter
2   teaspoons finely grated lemon peel
1   teaspoon fennel seeds, crushed

    Fresh thyme sprigs (optional)

Cook fennel bulbs in large saucepan of boiling salted water until crisp-tender, about 8 minutes. Drain; cool.

Toss fennel, bell peppers, olive oil and 1 teaspoon chopped thyme in large bowl to coat. Season to taste with salt and pepper. *(Can be made 1 day ahead. Cover and refrigerate.)*

Preheat broiler. Using mallet or rolling pin, pound each chicken breast between sheets of plastic to ½-inch thickness. Sprinkle with salt and pepper. Place chicken, skin side down, on broiler pan.

Watching closely, broil chicken 4 to 5 inches from heat source until golden brown and almost cooked through, about 5 minutes. Remove broiler pan from oven. Pour off any pan drippings. Using tongs, turn chicken over and broil until skin is golden brown and chicken is cooked through, about 4 minutes longer. Transfer chicken to platter. Tent with foil to keep warm. Pour off any pan drippings.

Working in 2 batches, arrange peppers and fennel in single layer on broiler pan. Broil until vegetables begin to brown and peppers are tender, 2 minutes per side. Transfer to platter with chicken.

Meanwhile, melt butter in heavy small saucepan over medium-low heat. Mix in remaining 2 teaspoons chopped thyme, lemon peel and fennel seeds. Season to taste with salt and pepper.

Drizzle butter mixture over chicken. Garnish chicken with thyme sprigs, if desired, and serve.

6 SERVINGS

REVISITING THE BUTCHER

Peruse the butcher's case or frozen foods section at a specialty foods market and you might feel as if you'd passed through a time warp into the future. Suddenly, all kinds of new meats—or rediscovered old meats or game—are appearing alongside the more familiar cuts. Keep an eye open for these up-and-comers.

◆ Buffalo: Also known as bison, this meat is lower in fat than beef, which it resembles in flavor.

◆ Duck: Once an item that had to be specially ordered, duck—particularly boneless duck breasts—may be found with increasing frequency in supermarkets.

◆ Ostrich: Now being farm raised in ever-growing numbers, this bird has meat with a nutritional profile resembling that of lean poultry. Yet its color, texture and flavor are more akin to those of beef.

◆ Rabbit: A meat long eaten in Europe, domesticated rabbit is a tender, flavorful white meat with a texture and taste like chicken's.

◆ Venison: Once considered primarily wild game, this flavorful, low-fat, fine-textured deer meat is now being farm raised.

◆ ◆ ◆

Peppercorn-crusted Muscovy Duck with Blueberries

◆ ◆ ◆

¼	cup sugar
2	tablespoons water
2½	tablespoons balsamic vinegar
1½	cups canned low-salt chicken broth
1	cup mixed dried fruit, cut into matchstick-size pieces
1	tablespoon minced fresh ginger
2	12- to 16-ounce boneless Muscovy duck breast halves with skin
4	teaspoons crushed mixed peppercorns
2	tablespoons (¼ stick) chilled butter, cut into small pieces
¾	cup frozen blueberries, thawed

Stir sugar and water in heavy small saucepan over low heat until sugar dissolves. Increase heat; boil without stirring until mixture is deep amber, occasionally brushing down sides of pan and swirling, about 8 minutes. Stir in vinegar (mixture will bubble). Add broth. Simmer until reduced to 1 cup, about 20 minutes. Remove from heat. Stir in dried fruit and ginger. Let stand 30 minutes.

Meanwhile, using fork, pierce duck skin (not meat) all over. Sprinkle with salt. Rub pepper over skin side of duck. Heat heavy large skillet over medium heat. Add duck, skin side down, and cook until golden and crisp, about 15 minutes. Turn over; cook to desired doneness, about 8 minutes for medium. Let rest 10 minutes.

Rewarm sauce over low heat. Whisk in butter a few pieces at a time. Stir in blueberries. Season with salt and pepper.

Slice duck breasts; serve immediately with sauce.

4 SERVINGS

Cider-marinated Duck Breast with Spicy Mango Chutney

◆ ◆ ◆

2   12-ounce boneless Muscovy duck breast halves with skin*

2   cups apple cider

    Spicy Mango Chutney (see recipe below)

Sprinkle duck breasts with salt and pepper. Place duck breasts in 13 x 9 x 2-inch glass baking dish. Pour apple cider over duck. Cover and refrigerate for 2 hours.

Heat heavy large skillet over medium heat. Remove duck from cider; pat dry with paper towels. Add duck to skillet, skin side down, and cook until skin is golden, about 15 minutes. Turn duck over; cook to desired doneness, about 10 minutes for medium. Transfer to cutting board. Let stand 8 minutes.

Cut duck breasts crosswise into thin slices; arrange on plates. Spoon warm chutney alongside and serve.

Available at specialty foods stores.

4 SERVINGS

Marinating the duck in apple cider results in a crisp, caramelized skin after sautéing. The spicy chutney pairs well with the sweet duck.

◆ ◆ ◆

Spicy Mango Chutney

2   tablespoons (¼ stick) butter

1   cup finely chopped onion

¾   teaspoon minced garlic

1   Granny Smith apple, peeled, cored, chopped

1   medium mango, peeled, pitted, chopped

¼   cup apple cider vinegar

¼   cup sugar

½   teaspoon dried crushed red pepper

¼   teaspoon dried thyme

Melt butter in heavy medium saucepan over medium heat. Add onion and garlic. Sauté until translucent, about 5 minutes. Add remaining ingredients. Simmer until mixture thickens slightly, stirring often, about 15 minutes. Season with salt and pepper.

MAKES ABOUT 1¼ CUPS

Turkey Cutlets with Leeks, Carrots and Peas

◆ ◆ ◆

A light sauté of turkey, tarragon, leeks, peas and baby carrots is a quick and easy way to bring the best of spring's harvest to the table.

8	ounces turkey cutlets, cut crosswise into ½-inch-wide strips
1½	teaspoons dried tarragon
2	tablespoons olive oil
1	cup thinly sliced leeks (white and pale green parts only)
¾	cup peeled baby carrots (about 3 ounces), halved lengthwise
1	tablespoon all purpose flour
1¼	cups canned low-salt chicken broth
¼	cup dry white wine
¾	cup frozen petite peas

Sprinkle turkey with 1 teaspoon tarragon, salt and pepper. Heat oil in heavy large skillet over high heat. Add turkey; sauté until no longer pink, 2 minutes. Using slotted spoon, transfer turkey to plate. Reduce heat to medium. Add leeks, carrots and remaining tarragon to drippings in skillet. Cook until leeks begin to soften, 3 minutes. Mix flour into vegetables; cook 1 minute. Gradually mix in broth and wine. Simmer uncovered until carrots are almost tender and sauce is thickened, stirring occasionally, 10 minutes. Add peas and turkey. Simmer until vegetables are tender and turkey is cooked through, about 2 minutes. Season with salt and pepper.

2 SERVINGS

Smoked Turkey Paella Salad

◆ ◆ ◆

⅓	cup (or more) purchased oil and vinegar dressing
½	teaspoon paprika
1½	cups canned low-salt chicken broth
¼	teaspoon crushed saffron threads or ⅛ teaspoon powdered saffron
¾	cup long-grain white rice
⅔	cup frozen green peas
6	ounces smoked turkey, cut into ⅓-inch pieces
½	cup coarsely chopped red bell pepper

Whisk ⅓ cup dressing and paprika in small bowl to blend. Bring broth and saffron to boil in heavy medium saucepan over high heat. Mix in rice. Cover and reduce heat to low; simmer until rice is almost tender, about 15 minutes. Mix in peas. Cover; cook until rice and peas are tender and broth is absorbed, about 5 minutes.

Transfer rice mixture to large bowl. Cool 5 minutes; fluff with fork. Mix in turkey and red pepper. Add dressing mixture; toss to blend, adding more purchased dressing by tablespoonfuls, if desired. Season salad with salt and pepper. Serve at room temperature.

2 SERVINGS

Cornish Game Hens with Orange and Honey

◆ ◆ ◆

1¼ cups orange juice

1¼ cups dry red wine

½ cup honey

2½ tablespoons soy sauce

¼ teaspoon ground cinnamon

⅛ teaspoon ground nutmeg

4 1½-pound Cornish game hens, giblets removed

3 small onions, quartered

12 garlic cloves, crushed

Preheat oven to 400°F. Whisk first 6 ingredients in medium bowl. Pour 2 cups sauce into medium saucepan. Reserve remaining 1 cup sauce for basting game hens.

Rinse hens inside and out. Pat hens dry with paper towels. Cut and scrape off any visible fat from hens. Sprinkle inside and out with salt and pepper. Place 3 onion quarters and 3 garlic cloves in cavity of each hen. Arrange hens on rack on large rimmed baking sheet.

Roast hens 10 minutes. Baste with reserved 1 cup sauce. Continue roasting until hens are golden and juices run clear when thickest part of thigh is pierced, basting often with pan juices and reserved 1 cup sauce, about 45 minutes longer.

Transfer hens to cutting board; tent with foil to keep warm. Transfer pan juices to 4-cup glass measuring cup. Spoon fat off top of pan juices. Pour pan juices into 2 cups sauce in saucepan. Boil until sauce is reduced to 1½ cups, about 12 minutes.

Discard onions and garlic from hen cavities. Cut hens in half lengthwise. Remove backbones. Spoon some sauce onto plates. Place hens atop; serve with remaining sauce.

8 SERVINGS

SOPHISTICATED DINNER FOR EIGHT

ASPARAGUS WITH
LEMON-HERB SAUCE
(PAGE 14)

CORNISH GAME HENS WITH
ORANGE AND HONEY
(AT LEFT; PICTURED ABOVE)

BAKED NEW POTATOES

YELLOW AND GREEN ZUCCHINI

CHARDONNAY

FRESH GINGER AND
CITRUS SORBET
(PAGE 210)

◆ ◆ ◆

◆ SEAFOOD ◆

Baked Halibut with Chopped Olive Salad

◆ ◆ ◆

½ cup chopped drained roasted red peppers from jar

⅓ cup chopped pitted Kalamata olives or other brine-cured black olives

⅓ cup chopped pitted brine-cured green olives

2 tablespoons fresh lemon juice

2 tablespoons minced fresh parsley

1½ teaspoons minced garlic

8 tablespoons extra-virgin olive oil

6 6-ounce halibut or sea bass fillets (each about ¾ inch thick)

¼ cup dry white wine

Combine first 6 ingredients and 6 tablespoons olive oil in small bowl. Season olive salad to taste with salt and pepper. *(Can be prepared up to 1 day ahead. Cover with plastic and refrigerate.)*

Preheat oven to 375°F. Oil rimmed baking sheet. Place fish on prepared sheet. Drizzle with remaining 2 tablespoons olive oil. Sprinkle with salt and pepper. Pour white wine around fish. Bake until fish is opaque in center, about 12 minutes.

Transfer fish to plates. Spoon chopped olive salad over fish, dividing evenly, and then serve immediately.

6 SERVINGS

◆ ◆ ◆

DINNER ON THE LAWN FOR SIX

PURCHASED HERBED CHEESE
SPREAD WITH SLICED
BAGUETTE TOASTS

BAKED HALIBUT WITH
CHOPPED OLIVE SALAD
(AT RIGHT; PICTURED OPPOSITE)

SAUTÉED SWISS CHARD WITH
SLICED GARLIC
(PAGE 146; PICTURED OPPOSITE)

STEAMED NEW POTATOES

SAUVIGNON BLANC

STRAWBERRY SUNDAES WITH
CRÈME FRAÎCHE ICE CREAM
(PAGE 210; PICTURED OPPOSITE)

◆ ◆ ◆

Grilled Sea Bass, Mango, Grapefruit and Avocado Salad

◆ ◆ ◆

A spice rub flavors the fish before it is grilled. The sea bass is served with a salad of greens, grapefruit, avocado and mango, the flavors balancing nicely with the fish.

◆ ◆ ◆

FISH

2	tablespoons paprika
2	tablespoons minced garlic
1	tablespoon olive oil
1	tablespoon chili powder
2	teaspoons dried oregano
1½	teaspoons ground allspice
¼	cup grapefruit juice
6	4- to 5-ounce sea bass fillets

SALAD

5	tablespoons grapefruit juice
¼	cup olive oil
2	tablespoons Sherry wine vinegar
1½	tablespoons chopped fresh mint
1	tablespoon chopped fresh ginger
	Nonstick vegetable oil spray
1	5-ounce package mixed baby greens (about 10 cups)
3	pink grapefruits, peel and pith cut away, segments cut from between membranes
2	large mangoes, peeled, pitted, thinly sliced
1	avocado, peeled, pitted, thinly sliced

FOR FISH: Grind first 6 ingredients in processor until almost smooth. Add juice and blend well. Season with salt and pepper. Sprinkle fish with salt and pepper. Rub 2 teaspoons spice mixture over each fillet; place on waxed-paper-lined tray. Refrigerate 2 hours.

FOR SALAD: Whisk juice, oil, vinegar, mint and ginger in small bowl to blend. Season dressing to taste with salt and pepper. *(Dressing can be made 2 hours ahead. Let stand at room temperature.)*

Spray barbecue rack with nonstick spray; prepare barbecue (medium-high heat). Spray fish with nonstick spray. Grill until just opaque in center, about 3 minutes per side. Transfer fish to plate.

Toss greens in large bowl with enough dressing to coat; divide among 6 plates. Arrange grapefruit segments and mangoes atop greens; drizzle with some dressing. Place 1 fish fillet alongside each salad. Top fish with avocado. Serve, passing remaining dressing.

6 SERVINGS

Cherry tomatoes tossed with red onion, jalapeño, basil and honey make a quick, zesty salsa for roasted snapper. Whip up this main course in less than half an hour. A salad of baby greens, orange slices and black olives is a nice go-with.

◆ ◆ ◆

Roasted Red Snapper with Cherry Tomato Salsa

◆ ◆ ◆

2	tablespoons olive oil
2	tablespoons chopped fresh basil
1	tablespoon fresh lime juice
1	cup small cherry tomatoes, halved
⅓	cup chopped red onion
1	teaspoon minced jalapeño chili with seeds
1	teaspoon honey
4	3- to 4-ounce red snapper fillets

Preheat oven to 400°F. Whisk oil, 1 tablespoon basil and lime juice in medium bowl to blend. Transfer 1½ tablespoons dressing to small bowl and reserve for fish. Mix remaining 1 tablespoon basil, tomatoes, onion, jalapeño and honey into dressing in medium bowl. Season salsa with salt and pepper.

Lightly brush small baking sheet with oil. Sprinkle both sides of fish with salt and pepper. Arrange fish on prepared sheet; brush with reserved 1½ tablespoons dressing. Roast fish until just opaque in center, about 10 minutes. Transfer fish to 2 plates. Spoon salsa alongside fish and serve immediately.

2 SERVINGS

Steamed Whole Red Snapper

◆ ◆ ◆

2   16- to 18-ounce whole red snappers, cleaned, scaled

16   very thin slices peeled fresh ginger plus 2 tablespoons chopped

16   very thin slices peeled garlic plus 2 tablespoons chopped

16   large fresh cilantro leaves plus 3 tablespoons chopped

3   tablespoons chopped shallots

3   tablespoons chopped lemongrass*

3   tablespoons chopped green onions

½   cup canned low-salt chicken broth

3   tablespoons soy sauce

2   tablespoons oriental sesame oil

2   tablespoons vegetable oil

    Cooked long-grain white rice

To begin, cut slits on each side of the fish. Place a slice of ginger and garlic, then a whole cilantro leaf in each slit; they will add flavor to the fish during the steaming process. Hold back the flaps to insert the seasonings more easily.

Sprinkle inside of each fish with salt. Using sharp cleaver or knife, make 4 diagonal slits on 1 side of each fish, spacing equally and cutting to the bone. Insert 1 slice of ginger, 1 slice of garlic and 1 cilantro leaf into each slit. Turn fish over. Make 4 diagonal slits on second side of each fish and insert remaining sliced ginger, sliced garlic and cilantro leaves. Arrange fish in 9-inch-diameter glass pie dish. *(Can be made 6 hours ahead. Cover; refrigerate.)*

Pour enough water into wok or large pot to reach depth of 1½ inches. Place bottom of 11- to 12-inch-diameter bamboo steamer over water in wok or open a steamer rack and place in pot. Place dish with fish in bamboo steamer (or on steamer rack). Curl tails if necessary to fit. Sprinkle 1 tablespoon each of chopped cilantro, shallots, lemongrass and green onions into dish around fish. Combine broth and 1 tablespoon soy sauce in cup and pour into dish. Bring water to boil. Cover bamboo steamer (or pot). Steam fish until just opaque in center at bone, about 18 minutes.

Before steaming, surround the fish with chopped shallots, lemongrass, green onions and cilantro. Then pour a broth and soy sauce mixture into the dish to flavor the fish as it cooks.

Meanwhile, combine sesame oil and vegetable oil in heavy medium skillet. Add chopped ginger and chopped garlic, then 2 tablespoons each of chopped cilantro, shallots, lemongrass and green onions. Stir over medium heat until oil is hot, about 3 minutes. Pour oil into small bowl; add 2 tablespoons soy sauce.

Using oven mitts as aid, transfer dish with fish to work surface. Using large spatula, transfer fish to platter. Spoon juices from dish over fish. Spoon some of seasoned oil over fish. Serve fish with rice; pass remaining seasoned oil separately.

*Available at Southeast Asian markets and some supermarkets.

4 SERVINGS

Grilled Tuna with Tarragon Mayonnaise

♦ ♦ ♦

¾   cup olive oil

3   tablespoons fresh lemon juice

2   large egg yolks

1   tablespoon water

2   tablespoons chopped fresh tarragon

   Additional olive oil

6   6-ounce tuna steaks (1 inch thick)

6   fresh tarragon sprigs

Whisk ¼ cup oil, lemon juice, yolks and water in small metal bowl. Set bowl over saucepan of barely simmering water (do not allow bottom of bowl to touch water); whisk constantly until thermometer maintains 140°F for 3 minutes, about 6 minutes total. Transfer to processor. With machine running, very gradually add ½ cup oil in thin steady stream (if oil is added too quickly, the mayonnaise will separate and become runny). Mix in chopped tarragon. Season mayonnaise with salt and pepper. *(Can be made 1 day ahead. Cover and refrigerate.)*

Prepare barbecue (medium-high heat) or preheat broiler. Drizzle additional oil over fish. Sprinkle with salt and pepper. Grill or broil about 3 minutes per side for medium. Transfer to plates. Top with mayonnaise. Garnish with tarragon sprigs.

6 SERVINGS

Halibut and Clams with Red and Yellow Bell Peppers

♦ ♦ ♦

3   tablespoons olive oil

1   cup chopped shallots

2   tablespoons minced garlic

2   tablespoons chopped fresh thyme

¾   cup dry white wine

¼   teaspoon crushed saffron threads

3½   dozen small clams, scrubbed

¼   cup bottled clam juice

1	cup finely chopped red bell pepper
1	cup finely chopped yellow bell pepper

4	6-ounce halibut fillets

1½	tablespoons chopped fresh cilantro
1½	tablespoons chopped fresh basil

Heat 2 tablespoons oil in heavy large pot over medium heat. Add shallots, garlic and thyme; sauté 2 minutes. Stir in white wine and saffron threads. Add clams. Cover and simmer over medium heat until clams open, about 8 minutes (discard any clams that do not open). Remove clams from heat.

Using tongs, transfer clams to bowl. Remove meat from shells; reserve meat. Strain cooking liquid and any accumulated clam juices into medium saucepan; discard solids. Add bottled clam juice to cooking liquid. Bring liquid to boil. Add peppers. Set aside.

Heat 1 tablespoon oil in heavy large skillet over medium-high heat. Sprinkle fish with salt and pepper. Add to skillet; cook until golden on bottom, about 2 minutes. Using spatula, turn fish over. Pour pepper mixture over fish. Cover and simmer over medium-low heat until fish is just cooked through, about 3 minutes.

Using slotted metal spatula, transfer fish to shallow soup plates. Add clam meat to skillet; stir just until heated through. Spoon over fish. Sprinkle with cilantro and basil.

4 SERVINGS

WHEN CLAMS CLAM UP

Clams (as well as mussels and other bivalves) are delicious when cooked fresh, but caution should be used when handling them to prevent a possible health hazard.

When fresh clams are purchased, they are still alive. A healthy, live clam will close its shell when handled before cooking, as part of a normal self-defense reaction. If a clam does not close after handling, it should not be cooked. The clam is probably dead and could be contaminated.

When a clam is cooked, the muscle used to close its shell should release. The two halves of the shell should part. If a clam does not open during cooking, it means that there was something wrong with that muscle all along. Eating that clam would be risky, so it's best to discard any that do not open before serving.

◆ ◆ ◆

Seafood Chowder with Dill

◆ ◆ ◆

8	ounces salt pork, trimmed, cut into ¼-inch dice
1¾	cups chopped onion
1½	cups chopped celery
¾	teaspoon dried thyme
½	cup finely crushed saltine crackers
2	10-ounce cans baby clams, drained, juices reserved
1¼	pounds white potatoes, peeled, cut into ½-inch pieces
2½	cups bottled clam juice
1½	pounds thick cod fillets, cut into ¾-inch pieces
1	cup half and half
½	cup whipping cream
¼	cup chopped fresh dill

Smoked Salmon Butter (see recipe below)

Stir salt pork pieces in heavy large pot over medium-low heat until crisp and golden, about 20 minutes. Using slotted spoon, remove salt pork and discard. Add onion, celery and thyme to drippings in pot. Increase heat to medium and sauté until vegetables are pale golden, about 10 minutes. Add crackers and stir until beginning to color, about 3 minutes. Add reserved juices from clams, potatoes and clam juice to pot. Bring mixture to boil. Reduce heat to low, partially cover pot and simmer until potatoes are almost tender, about 15 minutes. Add cod pieces; simmer until fish is cooked through and potatoes are tender, about 5 minutes longer. Add half and half, cream and clams. Cook until heated, about 5 minutes (do not boil). Mix in dill. Season with salt and pepper.

Ladle chowder into serving bowls. Top each bowl with heaping tablespoonful of Smoked Salmon Butter and serve.

6 SERVINGS

Smoked Salmon Butter

½	cup (1 stick) unsalted butter, room temperature
3	ounces smoked salmon, finely chopped (about ¾ cup)
2	tablespoons chopped fresh dill

Stir all ingredients in small bowl until well blended. Season to taste with salt and pepper. *(Can be made 1 day ahead; chill.)*

MAKES ABOUT 1 CUP

SEAFOOD DINNER FOR SIX

Cream of Onion Soup
(page 28)

Roasted Monkfish with
Fennel-Saffron Compote
(at right; pictured above)

Steamed Rice

Sautéed Spinach

Sauvignon Blanc

Pear Tartlets

◆ ◆ ◆

Roasted Monkfish with Fennel-Saffron Compote

◆ ◆ ◆

2¾ to 3 pounds monkfish fillets (about 5), well trimmed
4   tablespoons olive oil
2½ teaspoons minced garlic
¼   teaspoon (packed) crushed saffron threads

Fennel-Saffron Compote (see recipe below)

Using small sharp knife, trim all membrane and gray portions from monkfish fillets. Combine oil, garlic and saffron in large bowl. Add fish and turn to coat. Cover and refrigerate, turning occasionally, at least 3 hours and up to 1 day.

Preheat oven to 450°F. Arrange fish, with marinade still clinging, on rimmed baking sheet. Sprinkle with salt and pepper. Roast until fish feels firm to touch and is cooked through, about 15 minutes. Spoon Fennel-Saffron Compote onto plates. Slice fish on diagonal into ½-inch-thick medallions. Arrange atop compote.

6 SERVINGS

Fennel-Saffron Compote

4   tablespoons olive oil
4½ cups chopped fresh fennel bulbs (about 2 large)
3¾ cups chopped onions
1   tablespoon fennel seeds, crushed
3½ teaspoons minced garlic
1½ cups dry white wine
1½ cups canned low-salt chicken broth
¾   teaspoon (packed) crushed saffron threads

Heat oil in heavy large pot over medium heat. Add fennel, onions and fennel seeds; cook until fennel and onions are very tender, stirring occasionally, about 1 hour. Add garlic; stir 2 minutes. Add wine, broth and saffron; simmer until thick, stirring occasionally, about 20 minutes. Season with salt and pepper. *(Can be made 1 day ahead. Cover and refrigerate. Rewarm compote over medium heat, stirring often, before using.)*

MAKES ABOUT 4 CUPS

Pan-seared Tuna with Ginger, Miso and Cilantro Sauce

◆ ◆ ◆

2   tablespoons fresh lemon juice
2   tablespoons oriental sesame oil
2   tablespoons soy sauce
1   teaspoon black pepper
6   5-ounce ahi tuna steaks (about 1 inch to 1¼ inches thick)

Ginger, Miso and Cilantro Sauce (see recipe below)
Fresh cilantro sprigs

Whisk lemon juice, oil, soy sauce and pepper in small bowl. Place tuna in 13 x 9 x 2-inch glass baking dish. Pour marinade over; turn to coat. Cover and chill 3 hours, turning occasionally.

Remove tuna from marinade. Spray large nonstick skillet with vegetable oil spray. Heat skillet over high heat. Add 3 tuna steaks to skillet and cook about 3 minutes per side for medium-rare. Transfer tuna steaks to plate. Tent with aluminum foil to keep warm. Repeat with remaining 3 tuna steaks.

Transfer tuna to plates. Spoon sauce over. Garnish with cilantro.

6 SERVINGS

Ginger, Miso and Cilantro Sauce

1½   teaspoons oriental sesame oil
½   cup minced shallots
1   tablespoon minced peeled fresh ginger
1   cup canned low-salt chicken broth
¼   cup frozen orange juice concentrate, thawed
3   tablespoons rice vinegar
2   tablespoons yellow miso (fermented soybean paste)* or soy sauce
2   tablespoons chopped fresh cilantro

Heat oil in heavy small saucepan over medium-high heat. Add shallots and ginger and sauté 2 minutes. Add broth, orange juice concentrate and vinegar. Boil until mixture is reduced to ¾ cup, about 6 minutes. *(Can be made 1 day ahead. Cover and chill. Return to boil before continuing.)* Stir in miso and cilantro. Simmer 1 minute.

Available at Japanese markets and specialty foods stores.

MAKES ABOUT ¾ CUP

PACIFIC RIM DINNER FOR SIX

CUCUMBER, RADISH AND
GREEN ONION SALAD WITH
CHILI-LIME DRESSING
(PAGE 150)

PAN-SEARED TUNA WITH GINGER,
MISO AND CILANTRO SAUCE
(AT LEFT; PICTURED ABOVE)

STIR-FRIED SUGAR SNAP PEAS
AND BABY CARROTS

STEAMED RICE

JAPANESE BEER OR
ICED JASMINE TEA

FRUIT SALAD WITH
PAPAYA-MINT SAUCE
(PAGE 182)

◆ ◆ ◆

Tuna and Potato Kebabs with Basque Tomato Sauce

◆ ◆ ◆

18 small red-skinned potatoes
2½ pounds ahi tuna, cut into 1½ x 1 x 1-inch pieces
3 tablespoons sweet paprika
2 tablespoons olive oil
2 cups hickory smoke chips, soaked in water 30 minutes, drained
   Basque Tomato Sauce (see recipe below)

Cook potatoes in large pot of boiling salted water until tender, 15 minutes. Drain. Cool completely. Cut potatoes in half. Combine potatoes, tuna, paprika and oil in large bowl. Sprinkle with salt. Toss to coat. Alternate potatoes and tuna on metal skewers.

Prepare barbecue (medium-high heat). Place smoke chips in 8 x 6-inch foil packet with open top. Set atop coals 5 minutes before grilling kebabs. Grill kebabs until tuna is just cooked through, turning occasionally, about 8 minutes.

Spoon sauce onto plates. Arrange kebabs atop sauce.

6 SERVINGS

Basque Tomato Sauce

3 tablespoons olive oil
4 ounces smoked ham, cut into ¼-inch pieces
1 cup diced onion
1 cup diced green bell peppers
4 garlic cloves, chopped
½ teaspoon dried thyme
2 28-ounce cans chopped diced tomatoes in juice, drained
¾ cup dry Sherry

Heat 2 tablespoons oil in large saucepan over medium-high heat. Add ham; sauté until golden, about 8 minutes. Using slotted spoon, transfer ham to small bowl.

Add 1 tablespoon oil to saucepan. Add onion, peppers, garlic and thyme. Reduce heat to medium-low. Cover; simmer vegetables, stirring occasionally, 10 minutes. Add tomatoes and Sherry. Bring to simmer. Cover partially; simmer until mixture thickens slightly, stirring occasionally, 20 minutes. Stir in ham. *(Can be made 1 day ahead. Cover; chill. Bring sauce to simmer.)*

MAKES ABOUT 4 CUPS

Spinach Salad with Shrimp, Fennel and Bacon-Balsamic Vinaigrette

◆ ◆ ◆

In this attractive salad, grilled fennel wedges are tossed with spinach and tomatoes, then topped with marinated barbecued shrimp. A balsamic vinaigrette is added while still warm and then the salad is tossed to coat.

◆ ◆ ◆

8	tablespoons olive oil
1	tablespoon fennel seeds, crushed
1	teaspoon dried crushed red pepper
1¾	pounds uncooked large shrimp, peeled, deveined
12	bamboo skewers, soaked in water 30 minutes
2	fennel bulbs (about 12 ounces total), fronds chopped, bulbs cut into ⅓-inch-thick wedges
2	6-ounce packages baby spinach leaves
2	cups chopped seeded peeled tomatoes
	Bacon-Balsamic Vinaigrette (see recipe below)

Mix 6 tablespoons oil, fennel seeds and crushed red pepper in small bowl. Thread shrimp onto skewers. Place on rimmed baking sheet. Pour oil mixture over; turn to coat. Sprinkle with salt and pepper. Cover and refrigerate 30 minutes.

Prepare barbecue (medium-high heat). Brush fennel wedges with 2 tablespoons oil. Sprinkle with salt and pepper. Grill fennel until golden, about 3 minutes per side. Transfer to large bowl. Grill shrimp until opaque in center, about 2 minutes per side. Transfer shrimp to plate; tent with foil.

Add spinach and tomatoes to fennel. Toss with enough warm vinaigrette to coat. Divide salad among plates. Sprinkle with bacon reserved from vinaigrette. Remove shrimp from skewers and arrange around salad. Garnish with chopped fennel fronds.

6 SERVINGS

Bacon-Balsamic Vinaigrette

5	thick bacon slices, cut crosswise into ½-inch pieces
5	tablespoons olive oil
¼	cup balsamic vinegar
3	tablespoons minced shallots
1	tablespoon minced garlic
1	tablespoon brown sugar

Cook bacon in heavy large skillet over medium heat until crisp. Using slotted spoon, transfer to paper towels (reserve as garnish for salad). Remove skillet from heat. Reserve 3 tablespoons drippings in skillet; mix in oil. Whisk vinegar, shallots, garlic and brown sugar in small bowl. Add to drippings in skillet. Stir over medium-low heat just until warm. Season with salt and pepper.

MAKES ABOUT 1 CUP

Grilled Lobster Salad with Avocado and Papaya

◆ ◆ ◆

2   cups mesquite smoke chips, soaked in water 30 minutes, drained
4   1¾-pound live lobsters

9   tablespoons olive oil
½   cup orange juice
3   tablespoons fresh lime juice
1   tablespoon minced seeded jalapeño chili
1   tablespoon finely grated lime peel
1½ teaspoons finely grated orange peel

2   avocados, halved, pitted, peeled, cut into ½-inch pieces
4   medium tomatoes, seeded, cut into ½-inch pieces
1   large papaya, peeled, seeded, cut into ½-inch pieces

10 cups mixed baby greens

Prepare barbecue (medium-high heat). Place smoke chips in 8 x 6-inch foil packet with open top. Set atop coals 5 minutes before grilling lobsters. Bring large pot of salted water to boil. Working in batches, drop lobsters headfirst into water. Cover; boil 2 minutes. Transfer lobsters to work surface. Immediately split in half lengthwise, using heavy large knife. Crack claws.

Arrange lobsters, cut side up, on grill. Cover; grill 6 minutes. Turn lobsters over and grill until just cooked through, about 5 minutes. Remove from heat. Remove lobster meat from shells. Cool. Cut meat into ½-inch pieces. Transfer to large bowl.

Whisk oil and next 5 ingredients in medium bowl to blend. Season with salt and pepper. *(Can be made 1 day ahead. Cover lobster and dressing separately; chill. Rewhisk dressing before continuing.)*

Add avocados, tomatoes and papaya to lobster in bowl. Pour ½ cup dressing over; toss. Season with salt and pepper.

Toss greens in another large bowl with enough remaining dressing to coat. Divide among plates. Spoon lobster atop greens.

4 SERVINGS

◆ ◆ ◆

FIESTA MENU FOR FOUR

MARGARITAS

SALSA AND TORTILLA CHIPS

GRILLED LOBSTER SALAD WITH AVOCADO AND PAPAYA (AT LEFT)

LEMON ICE DRIZZLED WITH TEQUILA

SUGAR COOKIES

◆ ◆ ◆

Wine-poached
Mahimahi and Shrimp

♦ ♦ ♦

6   5-ounce skinless mahimahi fillets (each about 1½ inches thick)
2   teaspoons olive oil

3   cups bottled clam juice
1   cup dry white wine
½   lemon, thinly sliced
3   garlic cloves, peeled
¼   teaspoon dried crushed red pepper
½   pound uncooked medium shrimp, peeled, deveined

Fresh fennel fronds

Pat fish dry with paper towels. Sprinkle with salt and pepper. Heat 1 teaspoon oil in large nonstick skillet over medium-high heat. Add 3 fish fillets to skillet. Cook fish on 1 side only until brown, about 3 minutes. Transfer fish to plate. Repeat cooking with remaining 1 teaspoon oil and 3 fish fillets.

Combine clam juice and next 4 ingredients in heavy large saucepan. Cover and simmer until flavors blend, about 10 minutes. Working in batches, add fish and any accumulated juices to pan. Cover; simmer gently until fish is opaque in center, about 10 minutes. Using spatula, transfer fish to platter. Tent with foil. Add shrimp to liquid. Simmer until shrimp are just cooked through, about 2 minutes. Using slotted spoon, transfer to platter with fish.

Remove garlic and lemon from cooking liquid; boil until reduced to 1 cup, approximately 20 minutes.

Divide fish and shrimp among plates. Spoon cooking liquid over. Garnish with fennel fronds and serve.

6 SERVINGS

Scallops with Bell Peppers, Tomatoes, Avocado and Mango

◆ ◆ ◆

1	red bell pepper
1	yellow bell pepper
1	green bell pepper
12	cherry tomatoes
1	tablespoon olive oil
1½	pounds sea scallops
¼	cup fresh lime juice
¼	cup gold tequila
⅓	cup chopped fresh cilantro
⅓	cup chopped fresh basil
3	tablespoons chilled unsalted butter, cut into pieces
1	cup diced peeled pitted avocado
1	cup diced peeled pitted mango
	Fresh cilantro sprigs

Char bell peppers over gas flame or in broiler until blackened on all sides. Enclose in paper bag; let stand 10 minutes. Peel and seed bell peppers. Cut all bell peppers into matchstick-size strips. Set aside.

Arrange tomatoes on baking sheet. Broil until tomatoes begin to brown and blister, about 5 minutes.

Heat oil in heavy large skillet over high heat. Add scallops and cook 2 minutes. Remove from heat. Turn scallops over. Add lime juice to skillet, then tequila. Simmer until scallops are cooked through and liquid is reduced by half, about 2 minutes. Using slotted spoon, transfer scallops to plate. Stir roasted peppers, tomatoes, cilantro and basil into cooking liquid. Add butter 1 piece at a time, whisking just until melted. Return scallops to skillet. Season with salt and pepper.

Spoon scallop mixture onto plates. Sprinkle with diced avocado and mango. Garnish with cilantro sprigs.

4 SERVINGS

◆ ◆ ◆

A combination of yellow, red and green peppers provides lots of color and flavor in this delicious scallop main course. Diced avocado and mango add a unique tropical touch.

◆ MEATLESS ◆

Toasted Barley Salad with Corn and Grilled Mushrooms

◆ ◆ ◆

½	cup pearl barley
1½	cups canned vegetable broth
1	large poblano chili or green bell pepper
1	small red bell pepper
2	large plum tomatoes, seeded, chopped (about 1 cup)
1	cup fresh corn kernels
⅓	cup chopped fresh cilantro
¼	cup chopped green onions
2½	tablespoons fresh lime juice
2	tablespoons olive oil
	Nonstick olive oil spray
4	large portobello mushrooms, stemmed, dark gills scraped away
24	large spinach leaves

Place barley in heavy large saucepan. Cook over medium heat until pale golden, shaking pan occasionally, about 10 minutes. Add broth to pan and bring to boil. Reduce heat to medium-low, cover and simmer until barley is tender and broth is absorbed, about 35 minutes. Uncover and let barley cool.

Char poblano and red bell pepper over gas flame or in broiler until blackened on all sides. Enclose in paper bag and let stand 10 minutes. Peel, seed and dice poblano and red bell pepper.

Place barley, poblano and red bell pepper in large bowl. Add tomatoes and next 5 ingredients; toss to blend. Season salad with salt and pepper. *(Can be prepared 1 day ahead. Cover; refrigerate. Bring to room temperature before serving.)*

Prepare barbecue (medium-high heat). Spray mushrooms with nonstick spray; sprinkle with salt and pepper. Grill until cooked through, 4 minutes per side. Transfer to work surface; slice thinly.

Arrange 6 spinach leaves on each of 4 plates. Top with barley salad. Arrange 1 mushroom alongside each salad. Serve warm.

4 SERVINGS

Asparagus and
Swiss Cheese Soufflés

◆ ◆ ◆

10   thin asparagus spears (ends trimmed), cut into 1-inch pieces

2½ tablespoons butter

2   tablespoons all purpose flour

1   teaspoon dry mustard

⅔   cup milk

2   large eggs, separated

⅔   cup (packed) grated Swiss cheese (about 3 ounces)

¼   teaspoon salt

¼   teaspoon black pepper

◆ ◆ ◆

Eggs and asparagus are often teamed up in omelets or frittatas. In this unusual variation on that theme, asparagus spears are the secret-at-the-bottom-of-the-dish in these individual, cheesy soufflés.

◆ ◆ ◆

Preheat oven to 450°F. Generously butter two 1¼-cup soufflé dishes or custard cups. Divide asparagus pieces between prepared dishes. Melt butter in heavy medium saucepan. Drizzle ¾ teaspoon butter over asparagus in each dish. Reserve remaining butter in pan. Bake asparagus until just tender and beginning to brown, about 6 minutes. Maintain oven temperature.

Meanwhile, add flour and mustard to remaining butter in pan and whisk until smooth paste forms. Set over medium heat and whisk 1 minute. Whisk milk and yolks to blend in small bowl; whisk into flour mixture. Cook until sauce thickens, whisking constantly, about 2 minutes. Remove pan from heat. Add grated cheese, salt and pepper and stir until cheese melts.

Beat egg whites in medium bowl until stiff but not dry. Fold whites into warm cheese mixture in pan. Spoon all of soufflé batter over asparagus in soufflé dishes.

Bake soufflés until puffed and golden brown, approximately 14 minutes. Serve soufflés immediately.

2 SERVINGS

Portobello Mushrooms with Scrambled Eggs, Spinach and Roasted Red Peppers

◆ ◆ ◆

4	3½- to 4-inch-diameter portobello mushrooms, stems and gills removed
4	teaspoons olive oil
¾	cup chopped onion
1	tablespoon minced garlic
1	10-ounce package ready-to-use fresh spinach leaves
1	teaspoon chopped fresh thyme
1	7.25-ounce jar roasted red peppers, drained, finely chopped
4	large eggs

Preheat oven to 400°F. Arrange mushrooms, rounded side down, in 13 x 9 x 2-inch glass baking dish. Sprinkle with salt and pepper. Bake until tender, about 15 minutes. Transfer mushrooms to plate. Reduce oven temperature to 250°F.

Meanwhile, heat 3 teaspoons olive oil in large nonstick skillet over medium heat. Add chopped onion and garlic; sauté until tender, about 7 minutes. Add fresh spinach leaves; toss until wilted, about 3 minutes. Stir in chopped fresh thyme.

Arrange spinach in same baking dish. Top with mushrooms, rounded side down. Fill each mushroom with 2 tablespoons chopped roasted peppers. Place in oven to keep warm.

Whisk eggs in medium bowl to blend. Sprinkle with salt and pepper. Heat 1 teaspoon oil in medium nonstick skillet over medium heat. Pour eggs into skillet; stir until softly set, about 2 minutes. Fill mushrooms with scrambled eggs. Top each with 1 tablespoon peppers. Divide spinach and mushrooms among 4 plates.

4 SERVINGS

SIX DEGREES OF VEGETARIAN

An estimated 20 million Americans call themselves vegetarian, but only about 10 percent meet the strict definition of the word, meaning they don't eat meat, fish or fowl. So what about the rest of them, and what do you serve when they're coming for dinner? Here are the six most common types of vegetarians and what they will—and will not—eat.

◆ Pollovegetarians: will eat poultry.

◆ Pescovegetarians: will eat fish.

◆ Lacto-ovovegetarians: will eat eggs and dairy products.

◆ Lactovegetarians: will drink milk and eat other dairy products, but will not eat eggs.

◆ Vegans: will eat no animal products at all, including honey, eggs and dairy foods.

◆ Fruitarians: will eat only plant foods, such as fruits, nuts and some legumes, harvested in a particular way that allows the plant to continue living.

◆ ◆ ◆

SQUASH FOR ALL SEASONS

Fall and winter find winter squash at their peak, but some varieties are available in markets and at farmstands year-round. Here is a guide to the most common kinds.

◆ Acorn: Named for its shape, this squash has a green, tan or orange ribbed shell with orange flesh.

◆ Butternut: This popular squash is shaped like a bowling pin, with tan-colored skin and orange flesh.

◆ Delicata: The oval Delicata has yellow skin, green stripes and yellow flesh, which has a sweet corn-like flavor.

◆ Hubbard: With a hard lumpy shell and large irregular shape, the Hubbard can range in color from green to blue-gray to orange. The flesh has a yellow-orange color.

◆ Kabocha: The sweet orange flesh of the Kabocha is surrounded by a dark green rind marked with lighter green streaks.

◆ Turban: This yellow- or orange-fleshed squash gets its name from its shape: a large round base topped with a smaller section that resembles a squat hat.

◆ ◆ ◆

Butternut Squash and Noodles with Coconut, Lime and Cilantro Sauce

◆ ◆ ◆

1	tablespoon olive oil
1½	cups chopped onions
2	pounds butternut squash, peeled, seeded, cut into ½- to ¾-inch pieces (about 4½ cups)
1	cup canned vegetable broth
1½	tablespoons minced seeded jalapeño chili
1	tablespoon minced garlic
1	cup canned light unsweetened coconut milk*
2	tablespoons fresh lime juice
1	teaspoon Thai red curry paste*
12	ounces dried futonaga udon noodles (oriental-style spaghetti)* or linguine
½	cup chopped fresh cilantro

Heat oil in large nonstick skillet over medium-high heat. Add onions; sauté until golden, about 5 minutes. Add squash; sauté 4 minutes. Add broth, jalapeño and garlic; bring to boil. Cover; cook until squash is almost tender, about 5 minutes. Stir in coconut milk, lime juice and Thai red curry paste. Simmer uncovered until squash is tender and liquid is slightly reduced, about 4 minutes. Season squash mixture to taste with salt.

Meanwhile, cook noodles in large pot of boiling salted water until just tender but still firm to bite. Drain noodles. Return to pot. Add squash mixture and cilantro to noodles; toss to blend. Serve.

These ingredients are available at Asian markets and in the Asian foods section of some supermarkets.

6 SERVINGS

Baked Polenta with Sicilian Peperonata and Olives

◆ ◆ ◆

Nonstick olive oil spray
6	½-inch-thick slices prepared basil- and garlic-flavored polenta roll
3	tablespoons olive oil
½	cup chopped red onion
4	large plum tomatoes, chopped
1	tablespoon red wine vinegar
1	7- to 7.25-ounce jar roasted red peppers, drained, chopped
⅓	cup chopped pitted Kalamata olives or other brine-cured black olives
¼	cup chopped fresh basil

Preheat oven to 500°F. Spray baking sheet with nonstick spray. Brush both sides of polenta slices with 1 tablespoon olive oil and arrange on prepared sheet. Bake until polenta is crusty, turning over after 7 minutes, about 14 minutes.

Meanwhile, heat remaining 2 tablespoons oil in heavy large skillet over medium-high heat. Add onion and sauté 3 minutes. Add plum tomatoes and vinegar and cook until tomatoes soften, about 3 minutes. Add roasted peppers, olives and basil and simmer 2 minutes. Season sauce with salt and pepper.

Arrange polenta on plates. Spoon sauce over and serve.

2 SERVINGS

Peperonata is a mixture of bell peppers, tomatoes and onion used in Italian cooking. Here, it tops crusty baked polenta rounds for an easy meatless entrée. (Prepared polenta rolls are now available at supermarkets across the country.)

◆ ◆ ◆

Pan-fried Celery Root, Potato and Goat Cheese Terrine

Served as a light lunch dish or even as an appetizer, this sophisticated terrine features celery root, eggplant and goat cheese, in addition to fresh water-packed mozzarella. This soft, delicate cheese with a mild flavor is available at Italian markets and cheese shops. If unavailable, regular mozzarella can be substituted.

♦ ♦ ♦

1   1¼-pound eggplant, cut crosswise into ¼-inch-thick slices
1   1¼-pound celery root, peeled, cut crosswise into ⅛-inch thick slices
1   14-ounce russet potato, peeled, cut crosswise into ⅛-inch-thick slices
    Olive oil (for brushing vegetables)

2   large red bell peppers
12 large fresh basil leaves
2   3.5-ounce logs soft fresh goat cheese (such as Montrachet), cut into ¼-inch-thick slices
1   7-ounce ball fresh water-packed mozzarella, cut into ¼-inch-thick slices

    All purpose flour
2   tablespoons vegetable oil

Preheat oven to 400°F. Arrange eggplant, celery root and potato separately in single layers on 3 nonstick baking sheets. Brush both sides of vegetables with olive oil. Sprinkle generously with salt and pepper. Working in batches, bake until vegetables are tender, about 6 minutes for eggplant, 10 minutes for celery root, and 15 minutes for potato. Transfer vegetables to separate plates. Cool.

Char red bell peppers over gas flame or in broiler until blackened on all sides. Enclose in paper bag; let stand 10 minutes. Peel and seed peppers. Quarter peppers lengthwise.

Place 12 x 12-inch foil sheet on work surface. Arrange half of potato on foil, forming 9 x 9-inch square. Arrange half of celery root over potato. Arrange half of eggplant over celery root. Arrange basil over eggplant. Top with cheeses, then peppers. Press firmly to compress layers. Repeat layering with eggplant, celery root and potato.

Using foil as aid to lift vegetables and peeling foil away while rolling, carefully roll up vegetables as for jelly roll. Wrap terrine in foil. *(Can be made 1 day ahead. Refrigerate.)*

Freeze terrine until just frozen at edges, about 2 hours. Slice terrine through foil into eight 1-inch-thick slices (do not remove foil). Transfer to baking sheet; freeze 10 minutes.

Lightly coat cut sides of terrine slices with flour. Heat 1 tablespoon vegetable oil in each of 2 large nonstick skillets over medium-high heat. Add 4 terrine slices to each skillet; cook until golden and cheese begins to melt, about 2 minutes per side. Remove foil and serve.

8 SERVINGS

Grilled Fontina and Caponata Panini

◆ ◆ ◆

4   slices crusty country-style bread (each about 3½ x 5½ inches)
4   ounces thinly sliced Fontina cheese
6   tablespoons purchased caponata
1   medium tomato, thinly sliced
2½ teaspoons chopped fresh rosemary or 1¼ teaspoons dried
1½ tablespoons olive oil

Arrange 2 bread slices on work surface. Top each bread slice with ¼ of Fontina cheese, 3 tablespoons caponata and half of tomato. Sprinkle each with half of chopped rosemary, then salt and pepper. Top with remaining cheese and bread. Brush top and bottom bread slices with olive oil.

Heat large nonstick skillet over medium heat. Add sandwiches to skillet and grill until bread is golden brown and cheese melts, about 6 minutes per side. Transfer to plates. Cut in half and serve hot.

2 SERVINGS

◆ ◆ ◆

Fontina cheese and caponata (a chunky Sicilian eggplant relish available in cans or jars at most supermarkets) make a substantial meatless sandwich—big enough to call it dinner, even.

◆ ◆ ◆

White Bean and Vegetable Cassoulet

1	tablespoon plus 3 teaspoons olive oil
2½	cups chopped red bell peppers
1½	cups chopped onions
1	cup thinly sliced carrot
1	tablespoon minced garlic
8	ounces yellow crookneck squash, trimmed, cut into ½-inch pieces
4	ounces green beans, cut into 2-inch pieces
1	tablespoon ground cumin
2	teaspoons purchased harissa paste* or ½ teaspoon dried crushed red pepper
1	28-ounce can diced tomatoes in juice
1	15-ounce can cannellini (white kidney beans), rinsed, drained
½	cup chopped fresh basil
½	cup millet**
2	cups water
½	cup fresh breadcrumbs made from French bread

Cassoulet, a classic French dish of white beans and different meats, is reinterpreted here as a meatless entrée full of vegetables and topped with a crust made of breadcrumbs and a cereal grass called millet.

Heat 1 tablespoon oil in heavy large pot over medium heat. Add bell peppers, onions, carrot and garlic and sauté until tender, about 15 minutes. Add squash, green beans, cumin and harissa paste and stir 1 minute. Add tomatoes with juices and bring to boil. Reduce heat to medium and cook until mixture thickens slightly, stirring occasionally, about 12 minutes. Mix in cannellini and ¼ cup basil. Transfer mixture to 13 x 9 x 2-inch glass baking dish. *(Can be made 1 day ahead. Cover and chill.)*

Heat 1 teaspoon oil in medium nonstick skillet over medium heat. Add millet; stir until light golden, 5 minutes. Add 2 cups water; bring to boil. Reduce heat to medium, cover and cook until millet is tender and liquid is almost absorbed, 20 minutes. Drain millet. Transfer to bowl; cool. Mix in breadcrumbs and 2 teaspoons oil.

Preheat oven to 350°F. Sprinkle millet mixture evenly over vegetables in baking dish. Bake until vegetables are heated through and topping begins to crisp, about 35 minutes. Sprinkle remaining ¼ cup basil around edges and serve.

*Harissa *paste, a spicy red chili paste, is available at Middle Eastern markets and some supermarkets.*

**Millet is available at natural foods stores and supermarkets.*

8 SERVINGS

Welsh Rarebit

◆ ◆ ◆

2 tablespoons (¼ stick) butter
2 tablespoons all purpose flour
2 teaspoons dry English mustard
½ teaspoon cayenne pepper
⅔ cup Guinness
1¼ teaspoons Worcestershire sauce
3¼ cups grated extra-sharp cheddar cheese (about 12 ounces)
12 ¾-inch-thick country-style white bread slices, toasted

Melt butter in medium saucepan over medium-low heat. Add flour; whisk to blend. Cook 2 minutes, whisking frequently (do not let brown). Mix in mustard and cayenne. Whisk in Guinness and Worcestershire. Add cheese 1 handful at a time, whisking until melted before adding more. Stir until sauce is smooth.

Overlap 2 bread slices on each plate. Spoon sauce over.

6 SERVINGS

Zucchini Fritters

◆ ◆ ◆

5 tablespoons olive oil
3 medium zucchini, trimmed, cut into scant ½-inch pieces
3 large garlic cloves, chopped
¼ teaspoon dried crushed red pepper
1 cup all purpose flour
1½ teaspoons baking powder
1¼ teaspoons dried oregano
¾ teaspoon salt
¼ teaspoon black pepper
¾ cup whole milk

Heat 2 tablespoons oil in large skillet over medium-high heat. Add next 3 ingredients. Sauté until zucchini is brown, 8 minutes.

Stir flour and next 4 ingredients in medium bowl to blend. Add milk; whisk until thick batter forms. Stir in zucchini mixture.

Heat 1½ tablespoons oil in same skillet over medium heat. Drop half of batter by rounded tablespoonfuls into skillet. Cook until fritters are brown and cooked through, about 4 minutes per side. Transfer to warm platter. Repeat with remaining oil and batter.

MAKES ABOUT 16

This slightly spicy version of the classic English dish of melted cheese, beer and bread can be served as a light main course or a side dish. In Britain, it's likely you'd be served this as a separate course between the entrée and dessert.

◆ ◆ ◆

Eggplant with Tomato-Mint Sauce and Goat Cheese

◆ ◆ ◆

◆ ◆ ◆

This satisfying meatless main course features roasted eggplant rounds and just enough goat cheese to add a lot of flavor—but not a lot of calories, fat or cholesterol.

◆ ◆ ◆

Nonstick vegetable oil spray

2   1-pound eggplants, trimmed, cut into ½-inch-thick crosswise rounds

1½ tablespoons olive oil

½   cup chopped onion

2   garlic cloves, minced

1   28-ounce can Italian-style tomatoes

3   tablespoons chopped fresh mint

½   teaspoon dried oregano

½   cup crumbled soft fresh goat cheese (such as Montrachet)

8   fresh basil leaves, thinly sliced

Preheat oven to 500°F. Spray 2 large baking sheets with oil spray. Arrange eggplant rounds on prepared sheets: brush lightly with 1 tablespoon oil. Sprinkle with salt and pepper. Bake 10 minutes. Turn rounds over and bake until tender and golden, about 10 minutes longer. Remove from oven. Reduce oven temperature to 350°F.

Meanwhile, heat remaining ½ tablespoon oil in medium non-stick skillet over medium heat. Add onion; sauté until tender, about 5 minutes. Add garlic and stir 1 minute. Add tomatoes with their juices, mint and oregano and simmer until sauce thickens and is reduced to 1¾ cups, breaking up tomatoes with back of spoon, about 20 minutes. Season with salt and pepper.

Spoon half of tomato sauce into shallow 2-quart baking dish.

Arrange eggplant rounds atop sauce, overlapping slightly. Spoon remaining sauce over. Sprinkle cheese over. Bake until heated through, about 20 minutes. Sprinkle with basil.

4 SERVINGS

Acorn Squash Stuffed with Wild Rice, Hazelnuts and Dried Cranberries

◆ ◆ ◆

7   cups water
2   cups wild rice (about 12 ounces)

3   small acorn squash (each about 10 to 12 ounces), cut in half, seeded

2   tablespoons (¼ stick) butter
2   cups finely chopped onions
2   teaspoons crumbled dried sage leaves
2   tablespoons fresh lemon juice
½   cup plus 3 tablespoons dried cranberries (about 3½ ounces)
½   cup plus 3 tablespoons chopped toasted hazelnuts (about 3 ounces)
¼   cup chopped fresh parsley

Bring 7 cups water and rice to boil in heavy large saucepan. Reduce heat; cover and simmer until rice is tender, about 1 hour. Drain. Transfer rice to large bowl.

Preheat oven to 375°F. Oil baking sheet. Place squash, cut side down, on sheet. Bake squash until tender, about 40 minutes. Cool. Using spoon, scoop out pulp from squash, leaving ¼-inch-thick shell; reserve shells. Transfer pulp to medium bowl; set aside. Reduce oven temperature to 350°F.

Melt butter in large nonstick skillet over medium heat. Add onions; sauté until very tender, about 15 minutes. Add sage; stir 2 minutes. Add rice, squash pulp and lemon juice; stir until mixed, breaking up squash pulp into smaller pieces. Mix in ½ cup cranberries, ½ cup hazelnuts and parsley. Season with salt and pepper.

Divide rice mixture among reserved squash shells. Place in roasting pan. *(Can be made 6 hours ahead. Cover and chill.)*

Bake squash until filling is heated through, about 25 minutes. Sprinkle with 3 tablespoons cranberries and 3 tablespoons hazelnuts.

6 SERVINGS

VEGETARIAN DINNER FOR SIX

SPINACH SALAD

ACORN SQUASH STUFFED WITH WILD RICE, HAZELNUTS AND DRIED CRANBERRIES
(AT LEFT; PICTURED ABOVE)

ONION AND POPPY SEED FOCACCIA
(PAGE 165)

PINOT NOIR

RASPBERRY HOT FUDGE SUNDAES
(PAGE 213)

◆ ◆ ◆

Penne with Tomatoes, Olives and Capers

◆ ◆ ◆

1	tablespoon olive oil
5	teaspoons minced garlic
12	large plum tomatoes, seeded, coarsely chopped (about 5 cups)
¾	cup coarsely chopped pitted Kalamata olives or other brine-cured black olives
¾	cup tawny Port
1	4-ounce jar capers, drained
2	tablespoons chopped fresh basil
2	tablespoons chopped fresh thyme
1	tablespoon chopped fresh oregano or 1 teaspoon dried
1	teaspoon chopped fresh rosemary or ½ teaspoon dried
1	teaspoon dried crushed red pepper
14	ounces penne pasta
	Additional chopped fresh basil
¼	cup freshly grated Parmesan cheese

Heat oil in heavy large pot over medium-high heat. Add garlic and sauté until pale golden, about 2 minutes. Add tomatoes and olives. Sauté until tomatoes begin to release their juice, about 5 minutes. Add Port and next 6 ingredients. Simmer until sauce thickens slightly, about 6 minutes. Season sauce with salt and pepper.

Meanwhile, cook pasta in large pot of boiling salted water until just tender but still firm to bite, stirring occasionally. Drain. Transfer to large bowl. Pour sauce over pasta; toss. Garnish with additional basil. Serve, passing Parmesan separately.

6 SERVINGS

◆ ◆ ◆

DINNER ON THE PATIO FOR SIX

GREEN BEAN AND
MUSHROOM SALAD

PENNE WITH TOMATOES, OLIVES
AND CAPERS
(AT RIGHT; PICTURED OPPOSITE)

ROSEMARY AND THYME
BREADSTICKS

CHIANTI

POACHED PEARS IN RED WINE
WITH ANISE AND LEMON

◆ ◆ ◆

Spaghettini with Gorgonzola, Leeks and Shallots

In this satisfying pasta dish, spaghettini, which is a thinner version of spaghetti, is tossed with a mixture of onions, leeks, green onions and shallots, then topped with the creamy Italian blue cheese, Gorgonzola.

◆ ◆ ◆

4 tablespoons olive oil
2 cups finely chopped onions
6 cups chopped leeks (white and pale green parts only; about 6 medium leeks)
1 bunch green onions (white part only), sliced
½ cup chopped shallots

1 pound spaghettini

1 cup crumbled Gorgonzola or other blue cheese (about 4 ounces)

Heat oil in heavy large skillet over medium heat. Add chopped onions and sauté until tender and beginning to brown, about 10 minutes. Add chopped leeks, green onions and shallots; sauté until very tender, stirring often, about 10 minutes.

Meanwhile, cook pasta in pot of boiling salted water until just tender but still firm to bite. Drain well; reserve ½ cup cooking liquid.

Return pasta to same pot. Add onion mixture; toss to combine. Mix in reserved cooking liquid by tablespoonfuls if pasta is dry. Mix in cheese; season with salt and pepper. Transfer to large bowl.

6 SERVINGS

Tagliolini with Lemon-Parmesan Cream Sauce

◆ ◆ ◆

6 tablespoons (¾ stick) butter
6 tablespoons fresh lemon juice
1 tablespoon (packed) grated lemon peel
1 cup whipping cream
¾ cup (lightly packed) freshly grated Parmesan cheese (about 1½ ounces)

¾ pound thin pasta such as tagliolini or linguine

½ cup finely chopped fresh parsley

Melt 6 tablespoons butter in large skillet over medium-low heat. Add lemon juice and grated lemon peel and simmer 5 minutes, stirring occasionally. Whisk in whipping cream and ½ cup Parmesan cheese. Bring to simmer. Remove from heat. *(Can be prepared 1 hour ahead. Let stand uncovered at room temperature.)*

Cook pasta in large pot of boiling salted water until tender but still firm to bite. Drain pasta thoroughly.

Add pasta and parsley to sauce. Toss over medium heat until sauce coats pasta. Season to taste with salt and pepper. Transfer to bowl. Sprinkle pasta with remaining ¼ cup Parmesan cheese.

4 SERVINGS

Linguine and Clams in Ginger-Soy Broth

◆ ◆ ◆

1   cup (packed) fresh cilantro leaves
4   tablespoons canned low-salt chicken broth
6   teaspoons reduced-sodium soy sauce
6   teaspoons minced peeled fresh ginger
4   teaspoons oriental sesame oil
4   teaspoons minced seeded jalapeño chilies
2   teaspoons minced garlic
32   littleneck clams, scrubbed

12   ounces linguine, freshly cooked
½   cup finely chopped red bell pepper
¼   cup thinly sliced green onions

Preheat oven to 400°F. Place 2 large baking sheets in oven to heat. Cut 4 sheets of foil, each about 18 inches long. Place 1 foil sheet on work surface. Arrange ¼ cup cilantro on 1 half of foil. Top with 1 tablespoon broth, 1½ teaspoons soy sauce, 1½ teaspoons ginger, 1 teaspoon sesame oil, 1 teaspoon jalapeño and ½ teaspoon garlic. Arrange 8 clams atop. Fold foil over, enclosing contents completely and crimping edges tightly to seal. Repeat with remaining 3 foil sheets, cilantro, broth, soy sauce, ginger, sesame oil, jalapeño, garlic and clams. Place foil packets on heated baking sheets. Bake until clams open, about 20 minutes (discard any that do not open).

Divide linguine among 4 bowls. Open 1 foil packet over pasta in each bowl to retain juices. Sprinkle with chopped bell pepper and sliced green onions and serve immediately.

4 SERVINGS

BAKING IN FOIL

Baking in foil is a great way to reduce the fat used in cooking. Although the technique may sound complicated, it's really rather simple. It allows the true flavors of the foods to come through, while keeping the ingredients juicy and tender. Plus, the method doesn't require low-fat substitutes to make up for lost flavor, as some healthwise techniques do.

This cooking method is borrowed from the classic French technique of cooking in parchment paper, called *en papillote*. *Papillon* means "butterfly," and the cooking term is a reference to the traditional butterfly shape of the paper used to wrap the food. While both parchment and foil will yield the same results, baking with foil has two advantages over parchment: It is easier to work with, and it is easier to find.

When this technique is used in the recipe at left, the juices from the clams combine with spicy Asian flavors to make a tasty, low-cal sauce.

◆ ◆ ◆

Pasta with Artichokes and Asparagus

❖ ❖ ❖

6   large artichokes, trimmed, halved, chokes removed
¼   cup olive oil
2   garlic cloves, thinly sliced

2¾   cups canned low-salt chicken broth
1¼   pounds asparagus, trimmed, cut into 1½-inch lengths
1   tablespoon chopped fresh thyme

1   pound farfalle (bow-tie) pasta

⅔   cup freshly grated Parmesan cheese
     Additional grated Parmesan cheese

Quarter each artichoke half. Heat oil in heavy large skillet over medium heat. Add artichokes and sauté until golden, about 6 minutes. Cover and cook until almost tender, about 5 minutes. Add garlic and sauté 3 minutes. Transfer artichoke mixture to large bowl.

Place same skillet over high heat. Add broth and boil until reduced by half, about 9 minutes. Reduce heat to medium. Add asparagus and artichokes and cook until both are tender, about 5 minutes. Mix in thyme. Season to taste with salt and pepper.

Meanwhile, cook pasta in large pot of boiling salted water until just tender but still firm to bite, stirring occasionally.

Drain pasta. Add pasta and ⅔ cup cheese to artichoke mixture in skillet; toss to combine. Season with salt and pepper. Divide pasta among plates. Serve, passing additional cheese separately.

6 SERVINGS

❖ ❖ ❖

For tips on preparing artichokes, see the sidebar on page 21. Here, the chokes are removed, and the artichokes are cut into wedges and sautéed, before being mixed with asparagus and added to pasta.

❖ ❖ ❖

Mixed-Mushroom Lasagna with Parmesan Sauce

❖ ❖ ❖

     Nonstick vegetable oil spray

1   teaspoon olive oil
1½   tablespoons minced garlic
2½   teaspoons dried oregano
1   28-ounce can crushed tomatoes
⅓   cup dry white wine

1½ pounds mixed fresh mushrooms (such as button, crimini and small stemmed portobello), sliced

12 noodles from one 8-ounce package no-boil or oven-ready lasagna noodles
Parmesan Sauce (see recipe below)

¼ cup grated Parmesan cheese

Preheat oven to 425°F. Spray 13 x 9 x 2-inch glass baking dish with vegetable oil spray. Set dish aside.

Heat ½ teaspoon oil in large nonstick skillet over medium-high heat. Add garlic and oregano and stir 30 seconds. Add crushed tomatoes and wine and bring to boil. Reduce heat and simmer until sauce is slightly thickened, about 6 minutes. Season to taste with salt and pepper. Set tomato sauce aside.

Heat ½ teaspoon oil in another large nonstick skillet over medium-high heat. Add mushrooms; sauté until mushrooms begin to release juices, about 9 minutes. Season with salt and pepper.

Spread ⅓ cup tomato sauce over bottom of prepared dish. Arrange 3 lasagna noodles crosswise in dish. Spread ¾ cup Parmesan Sauce over. Arrange ⅓ of mushrooms over sauce. Spoon ½ cup tomato sauce over mushrooms. Repeat layering 2 more times. Top with 3 lasagna noodles. Spread remaining Parmesan Sauce over. Drizzle with remaining tomato sauce. Sprinkle with Parmesan.

Cover lasagna with foil. Bake 20 minutes. Uncover and bake until noodles are tender and top is golden, about 25 minutes longer. Let stand 10 minutes before serving.

8 SERVINGS

This lasagna uses the new no-boil or oven-ready noodles, which can be layered in the pan without cooking them first. It's a step that saves time—and a pot to wash. The Parmesan sauce would also be good over fish or a medley of steamed broccoli and cauliflower florets.

♦ ♦ ♦

Parmesan Sauce

⅓ cup all purpose flour

3 cups low-fat milk

¼ teaspoon ground nutmeg

¾ cup grated Parmesan cheese

1 teaspoon butter

Whisk flour in heavy medium saucepan to remove any lumps. Gradually add 1 cup milk, whisking until smooth. Add remaining 2 cups milk and nutmeg; whisk over medium heat until mixture thickens and boils, about 4 minutes. Remove from heat. Stir in Parmesan and butter. Season to taste with salt and pepper.

MAKES ABOUT 3 CUPS

To keep the potatoes from becoming gummy, press them through a ricer (or mash them) while still warm.

Mix in just enough flour to produce a dough that is soft and light in texture and only slightly sticky.

Use just a bit of flour on the work surface to prevent the dough from drying out. Apply only gentle pressure to keep the texture light.

Potato Gnocchi with Beef Ragù

◆ ◆ ◆

RAGU

½	cup olive oil
1¾	cups chopped onions
3	ounces pancetta* or bacon, finely chopped
2	ounces prosciutto, finely chopped
3	tablespoons chopped garlic
2	pounds ground chuck
4	cups beef stock or canned beef broth
1	ounce dried porcini mushrooms, broken into small pieces
1	tablespoon dried sage leaves
1	6-ounce can tomato paste
1	28-ounce can diced tomatoes in juice
3	cups (about) water

GNOCCHI

4	small russet potatoes (22 to 24 ounces total), peeled, cut into ½-inch pieces
1	large egg
2	tablespoons whipping cream
1¼	teaspoons salt
⅛	teaspoon ground nutmeg
1½	cups (about) all purpose flour
½	cup (1 stick) butter
	Wedge of Parmesan cheese
	Fresh sage sprigs (optional)

FOR RAGU: Heat oil in heavy large pot over medium heat. Add onions, pancetta, prosciutto and garlic and sauté until mixture begins to brown, about 10 minutes. Add ground chuck and cook until no longer pink, breaking up with fork, about 5 minutes. Add 1 cup stock, mushrooms and sage. Simmer until liquid is almost absorbed, about 4 minutes. Add remaining 3 cups stock, 1 cup at a time, simmering until liquid is almost absorbed before adding more. Mix in tomato paste, then tomatoes with juices. Simmer until meat is very tender, stirring occasionally and thinning with about 1 cup water every 30 minutes, about 1½ hours (sauce will be medium-thick consistency). *(Can be prepared up to 4 days ahead. Refrigerate uncovered until cold. Cover; keep refrigerated.)*

FOR GNOCCHI: Steam potatoes over boiling water until tender, about 12 minutes. Working in batches, press warm potatoes through ricer into large bowl (or place warm potatoes in large bowl and mash finely with potato masher). Cool until lukewarm, about 10 minutes. Add egg, cream, salt and nutmeg and blend well. Add 1½ cups flour and mix until soft and slightly sticky dough forms, adding more flour by tablespoonfuls if dough is too moist.

Turn dough out onto lightly floured work surface. Divide into 6 equal portions. Gently roll 1 dough portion between hands and work surface to ¾-inch-thick rope about 20 inches long. Cut into ¾-inch-long pieces. Roll each piece over wires of slender whisk or dinner fork to make grooves in gnocchi. Arrange gnocchi in single layer on floured baking sheet. Repeat with remaining 5 dough portions.

Cook ⅓ of gnocchi in large pot of boiling generously salted water until gnocchi rise to top and are cooked through and tender, about 5 minutes (check at 4 minutes). Using large strainer or slotted spoon, transfer gnocchi to large baking pan; arrange gnocchi in single layer. Cook remaining gnocchi in 2 batches. *(Can be prepared 2 days ahead; cover and refrigerate.)*

Melt butter in large skillet over medium heat. Add gnocchi and cook until heated through, tossing often, about 8 minutes.

Meanwhile, rewarm ragù over medium-low heat, stirring occasionally. Season to taste with salt and pepper. Ladle ragù into large shallow bowls. Spoon gnocchi over. Using vegetable peeler, shave Parmesan cheese over gnocchi. Garnish with fresh sage, if desired.

*Available at Italian markets and some specialty foods stores.

6 SERVINGS

Traditionally, gnocchi are grooved so that the sauce will better cling to them. Here, a slender whisk is an efficient tool to make grooves in each dumpling. Simply roll the gnocchi down the length of the whisk, pressing to make an imprint.

Gemelli with Shrimp, Tomatoes and Walnut-Parsley Sauce

4	cups fresh Italian parsley leaves (about 1 large bunch)
1	cup walnuts (about 3½ ounces), toasted
6	teaspoons chopped garlic
1½	teaspoons grated lemon peel
½	cup extra-virgin olive oil
1	pound gemelli or fusilli
2	tablespoons (¼ stick) butter
1¼	pounds medium shrimp, peeled, deveined
¼	cup fresh lemon juice
1	1-pint basket cherry tomatoes, stemmed, halved

Blend parsley, ¾ cup walnuts, 5 teaspoons garlic and grated lemon peel in processor until nuts are finely chopped. With machine running, gradually add oil and blend until coarse paste forms. Season sauce to taste with salt and pepper.

Add pasta to large pot of boiling salted water and cook, stirring occasionally, until just tender but still firm to bite.

Meanwhile, melt butter in heavy medium skillet over medium heat. Add remaining 1 teaspoon garlic; sauté 30 seconds. Add shrimp; sauté 2 minutes. Add lemon juice and simmer until shrimp are just opaque in center, about 2 minutes.

Drain pasta well; return to same pot. Add parsley sauce; toss until coated. Mix in shrimp and tomatoes. Season with salt and pepper; top with remaining ¼ cup walnuts and serve.

6 SERVINGS

One piece of *gemelli* consists of two strands of pasta—both about an inch long—twisted around each other to resemble a braid. These thick noodles are great for catching the juices in this garlicky entrée (opposite). If you can't find gemelli, fusilli will work just as well.

Fettuccine with Shiitake Mushrooms, Peas and Prosciutto

◆ ◆ ◆

3	tablespoons butter
6	green onions, thinly sliced
¼	cup minced shallots
1	pound fresh shiitake mushrooms, stemmed, caps sliced
½	cup dry white wine
8	ounces fresh peas, shelled, or 1¾ cups frozen peas, thawed
½	cup whipping cream
1	pound fettuccine
3	ounces thinly sliced prosciutto, cut into thin strips
	Chopped Italian parsley

Melt butter in heavy large skillet over medium-high heat. Add green onions and shallots and sauté until onions soften, about 2 minutes. Add mushrooms and wine. Cover skillet and cook until mushrooms are tender, stirring occasionally, about 6 minutes. Reduce heat to medium-low. Add peas and cream; simmer until peas are tender, about 5 minutes. Season with salt and pepper.

Meanwhile, cook pasta in large pot of boiling salted water until just tender but still firm to bite. Drain well.

Return pasta to same pot. Mix in mushroom sauce and prosciutto; season with salt and pepper. Transfer to large bowl; sprinkle with parsley and serve immediately.

6 SERVINGS

◆ ◆ ◆

In addition to the shiitake mushrooms called for here, look for fresh morels, porcini or even button mushrooms, all of which will taste great in this quick and easy recipe.

◆ ◆ ◆

Fettuccine with Broccoli Rabe, Tomatoes and Ricotta Salata

◆ ◆ ◆

2   bunches broccoli rabe (also called rapini),* cut into 1-inch pieces
12   ounces spinach fettuccine or pappardelle

½   cup extra-virgin olive oil
3   garlic cloves, thinly sliced
4   tomatoes, peeled, seeded, diced

4   anchovy fillets, drained, chopped
6   ounces ricotta salata (dried ricotta) or feta cheese, crumbled

Lots of garlic adds great flavor to this dish, which can be made with *pappardelle*, the wide thin noodles, or fettuccine, a convenient substitute.

◆ ◆ ◆

Bring large pot of salted water to boil. Add broccoli rabe and cook until stalks are crisp-tender, 3 minutes. Using approximately 4- to 5-inch-diameter strainer, transfer to large bowl. Return water in pot to boil. Add pasta and cook until just tender but still firm to bite. Drain, reserving ½ cup cooking liquid.

Meanwhile, heat ¼ cup oil in heavy medium skillet over medium heat. Add half of garlic; sauté 1 minute. Add tomatoes; cook until very soft, stirring frequently, about 5 minutes. Season tomato mixture to taste with salt and pepper.

Heat ¼ cup oil in heavy large skillet over medium-high heat. Add anchovies and remaining garlic; sauté 2 minutes. Add broccoli rabe; sauté 2 minutes. Add pasta and reserved cooking liquid and toss to heat through. Season with salt and pepper. Spoon pasta onto plates. Spoon tomato mixture around. Sprinkle with cheese.

Broccoli rabe is a leafy green stalk with scattered clusters of tiny broccoli-like florets. It is available at specialty foods stores and also at some supermarkets nationwide.

4 SERVINGS

Grilled Pizza with
Tomatoes, Corn and Cheese

◆ ◆ ◆

¼	cup warm water (105°F to 115°F)
1½	teaspoons dry yeast
1½	cups water, room temperature
2½	teaspoons coarse salt
3¾	cups (about) unbleached all purpose flour
	Extra-virgin olive oil
1½	cups grated Parmesan cheese (about 3½ ounces)
1½	cups grated Fontina cheese (about 6 ounces)
4	medium tomatoes, thinly sliced
1	cup fresh corn kernels or frozen, thawed
¼	cup chopped fresh cilantro or Italian parsley
4	teaspoons minced seeded jalapeños

Pour ¼ cup warm water into large bowl. Sprinkle dry yeast over; stir to blend. Let stand until yeast dissolves and mixture is slightly foamy, approximately 10 minutes.

Stir 1½ cups room-temperature water and salt into yeast mixture. Add 3½ cups flour, ½ cup at a time, stirring until slightly sticky dough forms. Knead dough on floured surface until smooth and elastic, adding more flour by tablespoonfuls if sticky, about 10 minutes. Oil large bowl. Add dough; turn to coat. Cover bowl with plastic wrap. Let dough rise in warm draft-free area until doubled in volume, approximately 50 minutes.

Punch dough down; turn out onto floured surface. Divide dough into 4 equal pieces; knead each briefly until smooth. Cover with towel; let rise until almost doubled, about 30 minutes.

Prepare barbecue (medium-high heat). Roll out 1 dough piece on lightly floured surface to 11 x 8-inch rectangle. Transfer to floured baking sheet. Brush top with oil. Place oiled side down on barbecue. Grill until bottom is golden, about 2½ minutes. Brush top with oil. Using tongs, turn bread over; grill until second side is golden, about 2 minutes. Transfer to baking sheet. Brush bread with oil. Repeat with remaining dough pieces. *(Can be made 4 hours ahead. Cover with foil; let stand at room temperature. Before continuing, prepare barbecue; use medium-high heat.)*

Sprinkle grated Parmesan and Fontina over breads. Top each with tomato slices, corn kernels, chopped cilantro and jalapeño. Drizzle with olive oil. Place pizzas on barbecue; cover loosely with foil. Grill until cheese melts, watching closely, approximately 2 minutes. Cut each pizza into pieces; serve warm.

8 SERVINGS

Pissaladière

◆ ◆ ◆

⅔ cup warm water (105°F to 115°F)
1 teaspoon sugar
1 envelope dry yeast
2 cups all purpose flour
5½ tablespoons olive oil
1 teaspoon salt

1¼ pounds onions, finely chopped (about 4 cups)
8 anchovy fillets, finely chopped

20 Niçois olives,* pitted
1 teaspoon chopped fresh marjoram

Combine ⅔ cup water and sugar in processor. Sprinkle yeast over; let stand until foamy, about 8 minutes. Add flour, 2 tablespoons oil and salt. Process until dough forms ball, about 30 seconds. Knead on floured surface until smooth and elastic, about 3 minutes. Oil large bowl. Add dough; turn to coat. Cover bowl with plastic, then towel. Let rise in warm draft-free area until doubled, about 1 hour.

Meanwhile, heat 3½ tablespoons oil in large skillet over medium heat. Add onions; sauté until beginning to brown, about 20 minutes. Stir in chopped anchovies.

Preheat oven to 425°F. Oil baking sheet. Punch down dough. Knead on floured surface until smooth, 2 minutes. Roll out to 12-inch round. Transfer to sheet. Pierce dough all over with fork.

Bake crust 5 minutes. Spoon onion mixture over, leaving border around edge. Sprinkle with olives and marjoram. Bake until crust is golden, about 15 minutes. Serve immediately.

*Small brine-cured black olives, available at specialty foods stores and also at some supermarkets.

4 SERVINGS

A pizza-like specialty of southern France, *pissaladière* is topped with onions, olives and anchovies. Try it for lunch or with a salad for dinner.

◆ ◆ ◆

SMOKED SAUSAGE

Salted, seasoned, stuffed into casings and cured with the savory smoke of smoldering wood, all manner of sausages develop wonderfully rich character that makes them delicious main courses in their own right or distinctive additions to other dishes. Check out some of these classics.

- Andouille: A peppery French or Cajun sausage made from pork and veal combined with wine, onions and spices. Ready to eat, it is excellent served hot or cold.
- Bockwurst: German sausage resembling hot dogs, made of veal or beef combined with pork and spices; cook in simmering water.
- Bratwurst: Fine-textured German sausage of pork or veal, served either grilled or fried.
- Kielbasa: Lean, precooked Polish-style sausage of seasoned pork and beef, often added to stews.
- Knockwurst: Fine-textured, plump, garlicky German pork-and-beef sausage, cooked in simmering water or on the grill.
- Mortadella: Large, fine, well-seasoned pork sausage, usually served cold in thin slices. From the Italian city of Bologna, which gives it the name by which it is better known in the U.S.

◆ ◆ ◆

Pizza with Sausage, Sauerkraut and Swiss Cheese

◆ ◆ ◆

1	tablespoon olive oil
1	large onion, sliced
1	teaspoon caraway seeds
1½	cups (packed) well-drained sauerkraut from jar, 1 tablespoon sauerkraut juice reserved
1½	cups (packed) shredded Swiss cheese
1	16-ounce purchased fully baked thick pizza crust
3	tablespoons Dijon mustard
8	ounces fully cooked kielbasa sausage, thinly sliced into rounds

Preheat oven to 425°F. Heat oil in heavy large skillet over medium-high heat. Add onion and caraway seeds and sauté until onion just begins to brown, about 7 minutes. Transfer onion mixture to large bowl. Mix in sauerkraut and 1 tablespoon sauerkraut juice. Cool to lukewarm, then mix in cheese. Season with pepper.

Place pizza crust on baking sheet. Spread with Dijon mustard and top with sausage, then sauerkraut mixture.

Bake pizza until cheese melts, topping begins to brown and crust is crisp, about 15 minutes. Transfer pizza to work surface; cut into wedges and serve immediately.

6 SERVINGS

Wild Mushroom Pizza

◆ ◆ ◆

1	medium-size red bell pepper
1	medium-size green bell pepper
1	tablespoon olive oil
½	pound assorted wild mushrooms (such as oyster, crimini, morel and stemmed shiitake), sliced
1½	teaspoons chopped fresh rosemary
1	10-ounce purchased fully baked thin pizza crust
1	cup shredded Fontina cheese
½	cup thinly sliced red onion

Char bell peppers over gas flame or in broiler until blackened on all sides. Enclose in paper bag; let stand 10 minutes. Peel, seed and thinly slice peppers. Set aside.

Preheat oven to 450°F. Heat oil in heavy large skillet over medium-high heat. Add mushrooms and rosemary. Cover skillet and cook until mushrooms are just tender, stirring occasionally, about 5 minutes. Uncover and simmer until any juices evaporate. Season mushrooms to taste with salt and pepper.

Place crust on baking sheet. Top with cheese, onion, peppers and mushrooms. Bake pizza until heated through and cheese melts, about 15 minutes. Serve immediately.

4 TO 6 SERVINGS

Spicy Spinach and Goat Cheese Pizzas

◆ ◆ ◆

1½   tablespoons olive oil, preferably extra-virgin
4   cups (packed) ready-to-use spinach leaves (about 6 ounces)
1½   teaspoons chopped fresh rosemary
½   teaspoon dried crushed red pepper
2   teaspoons fresh lemon juice
1   teaspoon grated lemon peel

2   6-inch purchased fully baked pizza crusts
1   3- to 3½-ounce package soft fresh goat cheese with garlic and herbs

Preheat oven to 425°F. Heat oil in heavy large skillet over medium heat. Add spinach; toss until beginning to wilt, about 2 minutes. Add rosemary and crushed pepper and toss 1 minute. Remove from heat; mix in lemon juice and peel.

Arrange crusts on work surface. Spread ¼ of goat cheese on each. Top each with half of spinach mixture, then drop remaining goat cheese over spinach by teaspoonfuls.

Place pizzas directly on oven rack. Bake until crusts are crisp and cheese on top begins to brown, about 10 minutes.

2 SERVINGS

◆ ◆ ◆

Packaged fresh spinach leaves and purchased pre-baked pizza crusts make this meatless entrée a snap to prepare. These easy pizzas are ideal for a midweek meal.

◆ ◆ ◆

·ON THE SIDE·

Poblano Potato Salad (page 158)
and Super Slaw (page 150).

Three-Chili Rice

♦ ♦ ♦

This side dish uses chili powder, jalapeños and *poblano* chilies (fresh green chilies often called *pasillas*) to turn ordinary rice into something special. Peas add color and interest.

♦ ♦ ♦

2	large poblano chilies*
6	tablespoons olive oil
¾	cup chopped onion
1½	tablespoons minced garlic
1½	tablespoons chopped seeded jalapeño chili
1½	teaspoons dried oregano
1½	teaspoons ground cumin
1	teaspoon chili powder
1½	cups long-grain white rice
2⅔	cups canned low-salt chicken broth
6	tablespoons crushed tomatoes with added puree
1¼	teaspoons salt
1½	cups frozen petite peas, thawed
6	tablespoons chopped green onions

Char poblano chilies over gas flame or under broiler until blackened on all sides. Enclose in paper bag; let stand 10 minutes. Peel, seed and chop poblanos. Set aside.

Heat oil in heavy large saucepan over low heat. Add poblanos and next 6 ingredients. Cover pan; cook until onion softens, stirring occasionally, about 10 minutes. Add rice; cook 2 minutes, stirring occasionally. Add broth, crushed tomatoes and salt. Bring just to boil. Reduce heat to low, cover pan and simmer until rice is tender and liquid is absorbed, about 25 minutes. Mix in peas and green onions. Remove from heat. Cover; let stand 10 minutes.

Fluff rice with fork and serve immediately.

Fresh green chilies, often called pasillas; *available at Latin American markets and some supermarkets.*

8 SERVINGS

Somen with Ginger
and Fresh Vegetables

◆ ◆ ◆

2	carrots, peeled
1	large zucchini
3	green onions
1	tablespoon vegetable oil
4	tablespoons matchstick-size strips fresh ginger
3	teaspoons chopped garlic
1	teaspoon oriental sesame oil
1¼	cups water
1	cup canned unsweetened coconut milk*
1	tablespoon reduced-sodium soy sauce
1½	teaspoons Thai red curry paste**
9	ounces somen**
½	cup finely chopped toasted peanuts
½	cup finely chopped fresh mint leaves

This spicy side dish is a wonderful culinary marriage of East and West: Noodles—which are staples in Thailand, Indonesia, Singapore and the Philippines—combine with vegetables cut julienne, a Western technique.

◆ ◆ ◆

Cut carrots, zucchini and onions into matchstick-size strips.

Heat vegetable oil in large skillet over high heat. Add 2 tablespoons ginger and 1½ teaspoons garlic; sauté until fragrant, 30 seconds. Add carrots, zucchini, half of green onions and sesame oil; sauté 2 minutes. Add remaining 2 tablespoons ginger and garlic; sauté until vegetables are crisp-tender, about 1 minute longer. Using slotted spoon, transfer sautéed vegetables to bowl.

Reduce heat to medium. Add 1¼ cups water, coconut milk, soy sauce and Thai red curry paste to same skillet. Stir until smooth. Simmer until sauce is reduced to 1¼ cups, about 6 minutes. Add sautéed vegetables and remaining green onions.

Meanwhile, cook somen in large pot of boiling salted water until just tender, about 2 minutes. Drain. Transfer to large bowl. Add vegetable mixture. Toss to coat. Sprinkle nuts and mint over.

*Unsweetened coconut milk is available at Indian, Southeast Asian or Latin American markets and many supermarkets.

**Thai red curry paste and somen—thin Japanese wheat noodles—are available at Asian markets, specialty foods stores and in the Asian foods section of some markets.

4 SERVINGS

COOKING WITH LESS FAT

Here are several techniques to help you reduce the amount of fat you use in cooking, without sacrificing flavor.

◆ Oven-frying: Foods that are "fried" in a very hot oven on a greased baking sheet have far fewer fat grams than their deep-fried counterparts. The high oven temperature sears the outside of the food and gives it a crisp brown crust. Use vegetable oil spray to coat the baking sheet. It adds flavor and aids browning.

◆ Grilling or Broiling: The searing heat releases fats from foods while locking in flavor and moisture. To minimize added fat, replace oil-based marinades with ones that use citrus juices or vinegar. Fresh vegetable or fruit salsas are great-tasting—and healthful—complements to grilled or broiled foods.

◆ Braising: Simmering foods in stock or other liquids that have been well seasoned with fat-free herbs will give tender and delicious results, without a lot of fat.

◆ ◆ ◆

Roasted Potatoes, Carrots and Shallots with Rosemary

◆ ◆ ◆

1¾ pounds medium-size red-skinned potatoes, cut into ¾-inch pieces
6   medium carrots, peeled, cut into 2-inch pieces
8   large shallots, peeled
3   tablespoons olive oil
1   tablespoon finely chopped fresh rosemary or 1½ teaspoons dried

Preheat oven to 400°F. Combine potatoes, carrots, shallots and oil in large bowl. Sprinkle with salt and pepper. Toss to coat. Transfer vegetables to roasting pan. Roast until vegetables are almost tender, stirring occasionally, about 45 minutes. Add rosemary and roast until vegetables are golden brown and tender, about 15 minutes longer. Transfer vegetables to bowl.

4 SERVINGS

Sweet Potato Fries with Garlic and Herbs

◆ ◆ ◆

      Nonstick vegetable oil spray
1½ pounds red-skinned sweet potatoes (yams), peeled, cut into ½-inch-wide slices, then again into ½-inch-wide strips
2   tablespoons olive oil

2   tablespoons chopped fresh Italian parsley
1   teaspoon chopped fresh thyme or ½ teaspoon dried
1   garlic clove, minced

Preheat oven to 500°F. Spray large baking sheet with vegetable oil spray. Toss sweet potatoes with oil in large bowl. Sprinkle generously with salt and pepper. Spread potatoes in single layer on prepared sheet. Bake until potatoes are tender and golden brown, turning occasionally, about 30 minutes. Transfer potatoes to platter.

Mix chopped parsley, thyme and garlic in small bowl. Sprinkle over sweet potatoes and serve immediately.

4 SERVINGS

Fresh Vegetable Medley

◆ ◆ ◆

6   ounces trimmed baby carrots, peeled
1   pound asparagus, trimmed, cut into 4-inch lengths
1   large fennel bulb, thinly sliced
8   ounces sugar snap peas, stringed
2   tablespoons olive oil
1   tablespoon chopped fresh tarragon

Bring large pot of water to boil. Add carrots and cook 1 minute. Add asparagus, fennel and peas; cook until all vegetables are crisp-tender, about 2 minutes longer. Drain vegetables. Return to pot. Add olive oil and chopped tarragon and toss to coat. Season with salt and pepper. Serve immediately.

6 SERVINGS

Butternut Squash and Sage Orzo

◆ ◆ ◆

3   tablespoons butter
1   cup chopped onion
1   garlic clove, minced
1   2-pound butternut squash, peeled, seeded, cut into ½-inch pieces (about 4 cups)
4   cups canned low-salt chicken broth
½   cup dry white wine

1   cup orzo (rice-shaped pasta)

½   cup freshly grated Parmesan cheese
2   tablespoons chopped fresh sage

Melt butter in heavy large skillet over medium heat. Add onion and sauté until tender, about 6 minutes. Add garlic and sauté until fragrant, about 1 minute. Add butternut squash and stir to coat. Add ½ cup chicken broth and wine. Simmer until squash is almost tender and liquid is absorbed, about 10 minutes.

Meanwhile, bring remaining 3½ cups broth to boil in heavy large saucepan. Add orzo. Boil until tender but still firm to bite, approximately 8 minutes. Drain orzo if necessary.

Transfer orzo to large bowl. Stir in butternut squash mixture, then Parmesan and sage. Season with salt and pepper.

4 SERVINGS

◆ ◆ ◆

In this hearty and surprisingly quick-cooking side dish, the rice-shaped pasta called orzo is combined with garlicky chunks of butternut squash, Parmesan and fresh sage.

◆ ◆ ◆

Saffron Rice with Peas and Garbanzo Beans

◆ ◆ ◆

2   cups shelled fresh peas or frozen, thawed

2   cups basmati rice
4   tablespoons (½ stick) butter
1   large onion, finely chopped
3   cups canned low-salt chicken broth
1   teaspoon salt
½   teaspoon saffron threads
1   15- to 16-ounce can garbanzo beans (chickpeas), rinsed, drained

Cook 2 cups shelled fresh peas in medium saucepan of boiling salted water until tender, about 5 minutes. Drain and reserve. If using thawed frozen peas, set aside.

Place rice in sieve. Rinse rice under cold running water until water runs clear. Drain. Melt butter in heavy large saucepan over medium heat. Add onion and sauté until tender, about 8 minutes. Add rice; stir 1 minute. Add broth, salt and saffron; bring to boil. Reduce heat to low. Cover and cook until rice is tender and liquid is absorbed, about 20 minutes. Remove from heat. Stir peas and garbanzo beans into rice. Cover and let stand 5 minutes. Transfer to bowl.

6 SERVINGS

◆ ◆ ◆

This recipe calls for basmati, a fragrant long-grain rice with a nut-like flavor. It's available at Indian markets and many supermarkets.

◆ ◆ ◆

Rosemary Mashed Potatoes

◆ ◆ ◆

3½   pounds russet potatoes, peeled, cut into 1½-inch pieces
3   tablespoons butter
¾   cup half and half
2   teaspoons minced fresh rosemary

Cook potatoes in large pot of boiling salted water until tender, about 25 minutes. Drain. Return to pot; mash until smooth. Mix in butter. Slowly mix in half and half. Add rosemary. Season mashed potatoes with salt and pepper. Serve immediately.

6 SERVINGS

Sautéed Fennel, Capers and Arugula

◆ ◆ ◆

1   teaspoon olive oil
1   1-pound fennel bulb, thinly sliced
1   cup thinly sliced leek (white and pale green parts only)
½   cup diced orange bell pepper
¼   cup drained capers
8   Kalamata olives or other brine-cured black olives, pitted, sliced
1¼   cups finely chopped fresh arugula

Heat olive oil in large nonstick skillet over medium-high heat. Add fennel and next 4 ingredients. Sauté until crisp-tender, about 3 minutes. Add chopped arugula and sauté 1 minute. Season to taste with salt and pepper and serve immediately.

6 SERVINGS

Rice with Green Onions and Olives

◆ ◆ ◆

1   lemon

1   tablespoon olive oil
1¼   cups thinly sliced green onions
3   cups water
1½   cups long-grain white rice
1   teaspoon salt
⅓   cup coarsely chopped pitted Kalamata olives or
     other brine-cured black olives
2   tablespoons chopped fresh Italian parsley

Using vegetable peeler, remove peel (yellow part only) from lemon in long strips. Set aside.

Heat olive oil in heavy medium saucepan over medium heat. Add green onions and sauté until soft, about 2 minutes. Add 3 cups water, rice, salt and lemon peel. Bring to boil. Reduce heat to low. Cover and cook without stirring until rice is tender and liquid is absorbed, about 20 minutes. Discard lemon peel. Mix olives and parsley into rice. Cover and let stand 2 minutes. Transfer to bowl.

6 SERVINGS

NOT YOUR TYPICAL BERRY

Normally associated with sweet summer fruits ripened on the vine, the term *berry* also applies to several savory ingredients that can add a powerful punch of flavor.

◆ Capers: These small immature flower buds of a shrub native to eastern Asia, but also widely grown in the Mediterranean, are pickled in vinegar or preserved in salt or brine, to be used as a piquant seasoning or garnish.

◆ Caper Berries: Comparable in size to olives and resembling huge capers, these are, in fact, the fruit of the bush that gives us capers. Pickled in the same way, they are generally used as a garnish.

◆ Green Peppercorns: The unripe berries of the pepper plant that, when matured, dried and ground, become the seasoning known as pepper, these have a sharp flavor that goes well with light meats, poultry and seafood. They may be found packed in water or pickled in brine, as well as dried.

◆ Juniper Berries: These dark-hued berries of the juniper tree contribute their distinctive, astringent flavor to gin. They are also used in marinades for game and pork.

◆ ◆ ◆

ALL ABOUT ENGLISH MUSTARD

Mustard has a long and colorful history in England, one that dates back to Roman times, with the Romans themselves bequeathing the gift of mustard to the Britons. The present was gratefully accepted and embraced by a populace that, to this day, prefers things (well, some things) hot. In fact, over the intervening centuries, the English developed a liking for an especially hot mustard.

Different forms of mustard, from the dried mustard balls of Shakespeare's time to mustard flour (which begat mustard paste, a common accompaniment to roast beef in the eighteenth century), have been developed over time, but none has been more popular than Colman's dry mustard, manufactured by one Jeremiah Colman beginning in 1814. More than 180 years later, the instantly recognizable yellow tins are still found all over the British Isles. Considered something of a national treasure, Colman's is made with hot *Brassica juncea* seeds and milder *alba* seeds, which are mixed with wheat flour and turmeric to turn it that familiar yellow color, or "mustard" as it's known in designer showrooms.

◆ ◆ ◆

Spinach with Roquefort Cheese

◆ ◆ ◆

2   tablespoons (¼ stick) butter
1   large shallot, finely chopped
2   10-ounce packages fresh spinach leaves
¼   cup crumbled Roquefort cheese

Melt 1 tablespoon butter in large pot over medium heat. Add half of shallot and sauté until tender, about 2 minutes. Add half of spinach and sauté until tender, about 5 minutes. Using tongs, transfer spinach to bowl. Repeat with remaining butter, shallot and spinach. Season to taste with salt and pepper. Sprinkle cheese over spinach and serve immediately.

4 SERVINGS

Mustard-glazed Carrots and Pearl Onions

◆ ◆ ◆

12   ounces pearl onions

3   tablespoons butter
1   tablespoon vegetable oil
1   pound peeled baby carrots
3   tablespoons (packed) golden brown sugar
2   tablespoons prepared hot English mustard (such as Colman's)
1¼   cups water

Cook pearl onions in small saucepan of boiling water 3 minutes. Drain. Cool slightly. Peel onions.

Melt 1 tablespoon butter with oil in large skillet over medium-high heat. Add onions and sauté until golden brown, about 5 minutes. Add carrots, brown sugar and mustard and stir 2 minutes. Add 1¼ cups water and bring to boil. Reduce heat to medium and simmer until vegetables are tender and liquid is reduced to thin syrup, stirring frequently, about 15 minutes. Add remaining 2 tablespoons butter and stir until butter melts and vegetables are coated, about 2 minutes. Season with salt and pepper.

4 TO 6 SERVINGS

Mashed Potatoes with Carrots

◆ ◆ ◆

3½ pounds russet potatoes, peeled, cut into 1½-inch pieces
¾ pound carrots, peeled, cut into 1-inch pieces
¾ cup whipping cream
3 tablespoons butter

Cook potatoes and carrots in separate medium saucepans of boiling salted water until tender, about 25 minutes. Drain potatoes and carrots. Return each vegetable to its own pan. Mash potatoes; stir over low heat to dry slightly, about 2 minutes. Mix in whipping cream and 3 tablespoons butter. Mash carrots coarsely in pan. Mix into potatoes. Season mixture to taste with salt and pepper. *(Mashed potatoes can be prepared 2 hours ahead. Let stand at room temperature. Rewarm over low heat before serving.)*

Transfer mashed potatoes to large bowl and serve hot.

6 TO 8 SERVINGS

Baby White Potatoes with Onions and Dill

◆ ◆ ◆

1 pound boiling onions (each about 1 to 1½ inches in diameter)

3 tablespoons butter

2 pounds baby white potatoes (each about 1 to 1¼ inches in diameter)

3 tablespoons minced fresh dill

Cook onions in medium saucepan of boiling water 3 minutes. Drain; rinse with cold water and peel.

Melt 2 tablespoons butter in large skillet over medium heat. Add potatoes; stir to coat. Cover skillet; cook potatoes until golden and almost tender, stirring occasionally, about 25 minutes. Mix in onions. Cover; cook until onions and potatoes are tender and golden, stirring occasionally, about 20 minutes longer. Mix in dill and 1 tablespoon butter. Season with salt and pepper. Transfer to bowl.

6 SERVINGS

◆ ◆ ◆

While there's much debate among food lovers about the best way to make mashed potatoes, for this recipe, you can't beat a good old-fashioned masher. It will work for the potatoes and the carrots, leaving each vegetable some texture in the process.

◆ ◆ ◆

Poblano Mashed Potatoes

◆ ◆ ◆

4   large poblano chilies* (about 12 ounces)

3   pounds russet potatoes, peeled, quartered

1   cup sour cream

¼   cup olive oil

Char chilies over gas flame or in broiler until blackened on all sides. Enclose in paper bag and let stand 10 minutes. Peel, seed and coarsely chop chilies. Set aside.

Cook potatoes in large pot of boiling salted water until very tender, about 25 minutes. Drain potatoes; return to pot. Mash potatoes until smooth. Mix in sour cream, oil and chopped chilies. Season potatoes to taste with salt and pepper. Transfer to bowl and serve.

*Fresh green chilies, often called pasillas; available at Latin American markets and some supermarkets.

6 SERVINGS

Sautéed Swiss Chard with Sliced Garlic

◆ ◆ ◆

2½   pounds red and/or green Swiss chard (about 4 large bunches)

¼   cup olive oil (preferably extra-virgin)

8   large garlic cloves, thinly sliced

Cut thick stalks and ribs from chard leaves. Chop stalks and ribs into ½-inch pieces. Cook stalks and ribs in large pot of boiling salted water until tender, about 5 minutes. Using slotted spoon, transfer stalks and ribs to plate. Add chard leaves to boiling water in pot. Cook just until wilted, stirring occasionally, about 3 minutes. Drain well. Squeeze excess moisture from leaves. Coarsely chop leaves.

Heat oil in heavy large skillet over medium heat. Add garlic and sauté until golden, about 2 minutes. Add chard stalks, ribs and leaves to skillet and sauté until liquid evaporates and mixture is heated through, about 5 minutes. Season with salt and pepper and serve.

6 SERVINGS

◆ ◆ ◆

A member of the beet family, Swiss chard has crinkly green leaves and celery-like stalks. It can be stored in a plastic bag in the refrigerator for up to three days. In this simple recipe, chard is parboiled, then sautéed with garlic for a flavorful side dish.

◆ ◆ ◆

Smoked Vegetables with Garlic Vinaigrette

◆ ◆ ◆

8   whole unpeeled garlic cloves
7   tablespoons olive oil

2   cups hickory smoke chips, soaked in water 30 minutes, drained
2   eggplants (about 1 pound each), cut into 3-inch chunks
2   zucchini, quartered lengthwise
2   yellow squash, quartered lengthwise
2   large red bell peppers, seeded, quartered lengthwise
4   carrots, quartered lengthwise

3   tablespoons Sherry wine vinegar

Prepare barbecue (medium heat). Toss garlic with 1 tablespoon oil in small bowl. Wrap garlic in foil, enclosing completely. Transfer to grill and cook until garlic is tender, about 25 minutes. Cool.

Place smoke chips in 8 x 6-inch foil packet with open top. Set atop coals 5 minutes before grilling vegetables. Meanwhile, combine vegetables in large bowl. Toss with 3 tablespoons oil. Sprinkle with salt and pepper. Grill until crisp-tender and golden, turning occasionally, about 8 minutes. Cool to room temperature. Cut into ½-inch pieces. Transfer vegetables to large bowl.

Press garlic to release from skins. Place garlic in processor. Add vinegar and 3 tablespoons olive oil. Blend until almost smooth. Season with salt and pepper. *(Vegetables and vinaigrette can be made up to 2 hours ahead. Cover separately. Let vegetables stand at room temperature. Refrigerate vinaigrette.)*

Toss vegetables with enough vinaigrette to coat. Season to taste with salt and pepper. Serve immediately.

6 SERVINGS

This recipe is based on a dish from Catalonia in northeastern Spain called *escalivada*, a mixture of vegetables roasted in the ashes of a slow fire. Plenty of wood chips add a smoky nuance here; the finished vegetables are offered in a roasted-garlic vinaigrette at room temperature.

◆ ◆ ◆

◆ SALADS ◆

Warm Wild Mushroom Salad

◆ ◆ ◆

4   tablespoons olive oil
2   tablespoons balsamic vinegar
½   teaspoon dried thyme
1   pound assorted wild mushrooms (such as oyster,
     crimini and stemmed shiitake), sliced
¼   cup chopped shallots
2   tablespoons minced fresh chives
4   cups torn mixed greens

Whisk 2 tablespoons oil, vinegar and thyme in small bowl.
Heat 2 tablespoons oil in heavy large skillet over medium-high heat. Add mushrooms and shallots; sauté until beginning to brown, about 3 minutes. Cover skillet; cook until mushrooms are tender, stirring often, 5 minutes. Uncover; simmer until any juices evaporate. Mix 2 tablespoons dressing and chives into mushrooms.
Toss greens with remaining dressing in large bowl. Top with mushroom mixture and serve immediately.

4 SERVINGS

Chopped Vegetable Salad with Feta and Olives

◆ ◆ ◆

1   large head romaine lettuce, finely chopped (about 8 cups)
4   medium plum tomatoes, seeded, finely chopped (about 1½ cups)
1   large cucumber, peeled, seeded, finely chopped (about 1¼ cups)
½   cup chopped red onion
¼   cup olive oil (preferably extra-virgin)
3   tablespoons red wine vinegar
1   cup crumbled feta cheese (about 4 ounces)
½   cup pitted halved Kalamata olives or other brine-cured black olives

Combine first 4 ingredients in large bowl. Drizzle oil and vinegar over. Season to taste with salt and pepper. Toss to coat. Mix in crumbled feta cheese and olives and serve.

4 SERVINGS

◆ ◆ ◆

Any mix of wild mushrooms will work in this delicious salad (opposite). The mushrooms are sautéed and served still warm on a bed of mixed greens that have been tossed with a balsamic vinaigrette.

◆ ◆ ◆

Super Slaw

◆ ◆ ◆

6	tablespoons rice vinegar
6	tablespoons vegetable oil
5	tablespoons creamy peanut butter
3	tablespoons soy sauce
3	tablespoons (packed) golden brown sugar
2	tablespoons minced peeled fresh ginger
1½	tablespoons minced garlic
5	cups thinly sliced green cabbage
2	cups thinly sliced red cabbage
2	large red or yellow bell peppers, cut into matchstick-size strips
2	medium carrots, peeled, cut into matchstick-size strips
8	large green onions, cut into matchstick-size strips
½	cup chopped fresh cilantro

Whisk first 7 ingredients in small bowl to blend. *(Dressing can be made 1 day ahead. Cover and chill. Let stand at room temperature 30 minutes before continuing.)*

Combine remaining ingredients in large bowl. Add dressing and toss to coat. Season with salt and pepper and serve.

8 SERVINGS

Cucumber, Radish and Green Onion Salad with Chili-Lime Dressing

◆ ◆ ◆

6	tablespoons rice vinegar
¼	cup sugar
1	teaspoon salt
2	English hothouse cucumbers, halved lengthwise, thinly sliced crosswise
2½	cups thinly sliced radishes (about 2 bunches)
1½	cups matchstick-size strips green onions (about 8)
	Chili-Lime Dressing (see recipe opposite)
1	tablespoon chopped fresh mint

Mix first 3 ingredients in large bowl to blend. Add cucumbers and toss to coat. Let stand 1 hour, tossing occasionally.

Drain cucumber mixture. Return cucumbers to large bowl. Add radishes and green onions. Toss salad with Chili-Lime Dressing. Sprinkle with chopped mint and serve immediately.

6 SERVINGS

Chili-Lime Dressing

¼ cup fresh lime juice

2 tablespoons soy sauce

1 tablespoon chili oil*

1 tablespoon (packed) golden brown sugar

1 teaspoon minced garlic

Whisk lime juice, soy sauce, chili oil, sugar and garlic in medium bowl to blend. Season dressing to taste with pepper. *(Can be made 6 hours ahead. Cover and refrigerate.)*

Chili oil is available at Asian markets and in the Asian foods section of some supermarkets.

MAKES ABOUT ½ CUP

Wild Rice Salad

◆ ◆ ◆

8 cups water

2 cups wild rice

1 red bell pepper, chopped

⅓ cup extra-virgin olive oil

⅓ cup chopped fresh Italian parsley

⅓ cup chopped fresh chives

3 tablespoons fresh lemon juice

3 tablespoons coarsely chopped fresh tarragon

2 teaspoons minced red jalapeño chili with seeds

2 teaspoons grated lemon peel

Bring 8 cups water to boil in large saucepan. Add rice; reduce heat to medium. Cook until just tender but not split, stirring occasionally, about 40 minutes. Drain. Rinse with cold water; drain well.

Place rice in large bowl. Mix remaining ingredients into rice. Season with salt and pepper. *(Can be made 2 hours ahead. Cover; let salad stand at room temperature.)*

6 SERVINGS

◆ ◆ ◆

Wild rice takes the idea of rice salad beyond the expected—without complicating the recipe. Red jalapeño chilies give it a real kick.

◆ ◆ ◆

BISTRO COOKING

Nowadays, the term *bistro* is applied to just about any restaurant that serves generous portions of well-cooked, casual food in relaxed surroundings. The word, however, originally described nineteenth-century French wine taverns that offered fast, reasonably priced meals to local working people.

Bistro fare might best be described as humble, were it not for the fact that it is cooked so very well. Simple salads, such as the trio on this page, could begin a meal. Pâtés and terrines are more favorite starters, along with robust soups of all kinds.

Many bistro dishes rely on quick cooking, from rapidly sautéed fish fillets to pan-fried steaks or chicken breasts. Still others are the sort that only improve in flavor and texture with long, untended simmering: braises and stews of inexpensive cuts, sometimes extended with dried beans.

The simplicity of bistro fare extends to dessert as well, which might be a piece of fruit and cheese. Custards, rustic pastries, a homemade ice cream or a soufflé that bakes while coffee is savored—all end the bistro meal in the same satisfying spirit with which it began.

◆ ◆ ◆

Trio of Salads

◆ ◆ ◆

5	2- to 2½-inch-diameter beets, tops trimmed
3	tablespoons minced fresh chives
	Shallot-Mustard Dressing (see recipe below)
3	cups grated peeled celery root (from about one 1¼-pound celery root)
1	tablespoon fresh lemon juice
1	tablespoon fresh minced parsley
½	teaspoon celery salt
3	cups grated peeled carrots
2	tablespoons minced fresh tarragon

Cook beets in pot of boiling salted water until tender when pierced with small sharp knife, about 30 minutes. Drain thoroughly. Cool beets. Peel and grate beets.

Mix beets, chives and ¼ cup Shallot-Mustard Dressing in medium bowl. Combine celery root, lemon juice, parsley and celery salt in second medium bowl. Mix in ¼ cup dressing. Mix carrots, tarragon and ¼ cup dressing in third medium bowl. Season each salad with salt and pepper. Cover and chill salads at least 1 hour. *(Can be prepared 1 day ahead. Keep chilled.)*

Arrange salads on platter and serve immediately.

4 SERVINGS

Shallot-Mustard Dressing

⅓	cup minced shallots
¼	cup red wine vinegar
1	tablespoon Dijon mustard
1	small garlic clove, pressed
½	cup olive oil

Whisk shallots, vinegar, mustard and garlic in small bowl to blend. Gradually whisk in olive oil.

MAKES ABOUT 1 CUP

Spinach and Radish Salad

◆ ◆ ◆

3   tablespoons olive oil
2   tablespoons fresh lemon juice
1   large shallot, minced

1   6-ounce package baby spinach leaves
1   large fennel bulb, trimmed, quartered lengthwise, cored,
    thinly sliced crosswise
1   bunch radishes, sliced
¾   cup crumbled feta cheese

Whisk oil, lemon juice and shallot in small bowl to blend. Season dressing to taste with salt and pepper.

Combine spinach, fennel and radishes in large shallow bowl. Add dressing and toss to coat. Sprinkle feta cheese over and serve.

4 SERVINGS

Beet, Red Onion, Caper and Mint Salad

◆ ◆ ◆

12 medium beets, tops trimmed
8   tablespoons extra-virgin olive oil

2   small red onions, peeled, very thinly sliced
½   cup chopped fresh mint
¼   cup balsamic vinegar
3   tablespoons drained capers

Preheat oven to 400°F. Place beets in large roasting pan. Add enough water to come 1 inch up sides of beets. Drizzle with 3 tablespoons oil. Sprinkle with salt and pepper. Cover with foil; bake until tender, approximately 50 minutes. Using tongs, transfer beets to bowl; cool completely. Peel beets.

Cut beets into 1-inch chunks. Place in large bowl. Add onions, mint, vinegar, capers and 5 tablespoons oil; toss well. Season salad to taste with salt and pepper and serve.

6 SERVINGS

◆ ◆ ◆

Beet salads are not uncommon in England, but this recipe takes the typical version and revives it with fresh beets roasted until rich and flavorful. Red onions, capers, balsamic vinegar and fresh mint add interest.

◆ ◆ ◆

Warm Green Bean Salad with Pine Nuts and Basil

◆ ◆ ◆

1½   pounds slender green beans, trimmed

2   tablespoons olive oil
¼   cup pine nuts (about 1½ ounces)
2   garlic cloves, minced
18   large fresh basil leaves, chopped

Cook beans in large pot of boiling water until crisp-tender, about 5 minutes. Drain. Place beans in bowl of ice water to cool. Drain well. Pat dry with paper towels. *(Can be made 1 day ahead. Wrap green beans in paper towels and refrigerate.)*

Heat oil in heavy large skillet over medium-low heat. Add pine nuts and sauté until light brown, about 6 minutes. Add garlic; stir 1 minute. Add green beans to skillet; sauté until heated through, about 5 minutes. Stir in basil. Season with salt and pepper. Transfer salad to bowl and serve immediately.

6 SERVINGS

Escarole Salad with Shiitake Mushrooms and Pancetta

◆ ◆ ◆

5   tablespoons olive oil
4   ounces fresh shiitake mushrooms, stemmed, caps sliced ½ inch thick

1   ¼-inch-thick slice pancetta,* chopped

2   tablespoons red wine vinegar
1   tablespoon Worcestershire sauce
1   tablespoon tomato paste
2   teaspoons Dijon mustard
1   tablespoon brandy
1   large head escarole, cut into 1-inch pieces (about 8 cups)

Heat 1 tablespoon oil in heavy medium skillet over medium-high heat. Add mushrooms and sauté until tender, about 2 minutes. Sprinkle with salt and pepper. Using slotted spoon, transfer mushrooms to paper towels; reserve mushrooms.

◆ ◆ ◆

Italian bacon, called pancetta, is a wonderful addition to this easy and innovative side-dish salad. Serve it warm for the best flavor.

◆ ◆ ◆

Heat 1 tablespoon oil in same skillet over medium-high heat. Add pancetta and sauté until crisp, about 2 minutes. Remove skillet from heat. Using slotted spoon, transfer pancetta to paper towels to drain; reserve pancetta.

Carefully whisk vinegar into drippings in same skillet. Bring to simmer over medium heat, scraping up any browned bits. Add Worcestershire sauce, tomato paste, mustard and 3 tablespoons oil, then brandy. Bring to simmer. Place escarole in large bowl; pour warm vinaigrette over. Toss to coat. Mix in reserved mushrooms and pancetta. Season with salt and pepper.

Pancetta, Italian bacon cured in salt, is available at Italian markets and some specialty foods stores.

4 SERVINGS

Smoky Bean Salad

◆ ◆ ◆

1½	pounds green beans, cut diagonally into 1-inch pieces
1	15- to 16-ounce can black beans, drained
1	15- to 16-ounce can red kidney beans, drained
9	bacon slices, cut into ½-inch pieces
6	tablespoons white wine vinegar
¼	cup vegetable oil
¼	cup minced seeded jalapeño chilies
3	tablespoons Dijon mustard
2	tablespoons (packed) golden brown sugar

Cook green beans in large pot of boiling salted water until crisp-tender, about 4 minutes. Drain beans; pat dry. Transfer green beans to large bowl. Add black beans and kidney beans to cooked green beans. Refrigerate all beans until cold.

Sauté bacon in heavy medium skillet over medium-high heat until crisp, about 5 minutes. Using slotted spoon, transfer bacon to paper towels to drain. Transfer 2 tablespoons drippings from skillet to medium bowl (discard remaining drippings). Add vinegar and remaining ingredients; whisk to blend. Season with salt and pepper.

Toss beans with enough dressing to coat. *(Can be prepared 8 hours ahead. Cover and refrigerate.)* Sprinkle with reserved bacon.

6 SERVINGS

Here, the typical succotash ingredients—lima beans, corn and bell peppers—flavor a salad instead of the hot side dish. Canned or frozen corn kernels work just as well as fresh, making this recipe seasonless.

◆ ◆ ◆

Creamy Succotash Salad

◆ ◆ ◆

⅔ cup mayonnaise

6 tablespoons buttermilk

4 teaspoons Dijon mustard

4 teaspoons fresh lemon juice

4 teaspoons sugar

½ teaspoon hot pepper sauce

2 large red bell peppers

3 cups frozen baby lima beans, thawed (from two 10-ounce packages)

5 cups frozen corn kernels, thawed, drained (about 24 ounces)

⅔ cup thinly sliced green onions

Whisk first 6 ingredients in medium bowl to blend. Season dressing to taste with salt and pepper.

Char bell peppers over gas flame or in broiler until blackened on all sides. Enclose peppers in paper bag; let stand 10 minutes. Peel, seed and coarsely chop peppers. Transfer to large bowl.

Cook lima beans in large pot of boiling salted water until heated through, about 2 minutes. Drain beans; cool.

Transfer beans to bowl with bell peppers. Mix in corn and green onions. Toss salad with enough dressing to coat. Season to taste with salt and pepper. *(Can be made 6 hours ahead. Cover and refrigerate. Serve cold or at room temperature.)*

8 SERVINGS

Endive, Arugula and Apple Salad with White Wine Vinaigrette

◆ ◆ ◆

2 cups dry white wine (such as Viognier or Gewürztraminer)

6 tablespoons extra-virgin olive oil

3 tablespoons white wine vinegar

1	small head escarole, torn into 1½-inch pieces
1	medium head Belgian endive, cut into 1-inch pieces
1	small bunch arugula, stemmed, cut into 1½-inch pieces
1	stalk celery, thinly sliced on diagonal
1	Red Delicious apple, halved, cored, thinly sliced
½	cup pecans, toasted
⅓	cup shaved Parmesan cheese

Boil wine in heavy medium saucepan until reduced to 3 tablespoons, about 13 minutes. Pour into small bowl; cool. Whisk in oil and vinegar. Season vinaigrette with salt and pepper.

Toss escarole, endive, arugula and celery in large bowl. Add apple, pecans and shaved Parmesan. Toss salad with enough vinaigrette to coat and serve immediately.

6 SERVINGS

Romaine Salad with Thousand Island Dressing

◆ ◆ ◆

1¼	cups mayonnaise
⅓	cup bottled chili sauce
¼	cup chopped drained pimiento
1	large hard-boiled egg, shelled, finely chopped
3	tablespoons finely chopped dill pickle
2	tablespoons Dijon mustard
2	tablespoons drained capers
2	tablespoons chopped green onion
	Hot pepper sauce
2	medium heads romaine lettuce, coarsely chopped (about 16 cups)

Combine first 8 ingredients in medium bowl and whisk to blend. Season dressing to taste with hot pepper sauce, salt and pepper. *(Can be prepared 3 days ahead. Cover and refrigerate.)*

Place lettuce in large bowl. Toss with enough dressing to coat.

6 SERVINGS

◆ ◆ ◆

Apple slices and toasted pecans add crunch to this salad; shaved Parmesan cheese lends a terrific flavor boost. (To get "shaves" of Parmesan, run a vegetable peeler over the top of a chunk of the cheese, after it has warmed up a little. Be careful to keep the shavings as thin as possible.)

◆ ◆ ◆

Spicy Sesame Noodle, Green Bean and Carrot Salad

❖ ❖ ❖

The dressing is packed with intense flavors—so only a small amount of oil is necessary, making this noodle salad lighter than most.

❖ ❖ ❖

¼	cup fresh lime juice
3	tablespoons canola oil
3	tablespoons soy sauce
2	tablespoons (packed) dark brown sugar
1	tablespoon oriental sesame oil
1	tablespoon minced garlic
1	tablespoon grated orange peel
2	small serrano chilies, stemmed, thinly sliced into rounds
9	ounces green beans, trimmed, cut diagonally into ½-inch pieces
1	9-ounce package fresh linguine
2	cups shredded peeled carrots
1	cup thinly sliced green onions

Stir first 8 ingredients in medium bowl to blend. Season dressing with salt and pepper. Let stand 30 minutes to blend flavors.

Cook green beans in large pot of boiling salted water until crisp-tender, about 2 minutes. Using slotted spoon, transfer beans to cold water to cool. Drain well. Pat dry with paper towels.

Return water to boil. Add pasta and cook until just tender but still firm to bite, stirring often, about 2 minutes. Drain. Rinse pasta under cold water. Drain well.

Combine green beans, pasta, carrots, green onions and dressing in large bowl. Toss to coat. Season with salt and pepper. *(Can be made 6 hours ahead. Cover and refrigerate.)*

6 SERVINGS

Poblano Potato Salad

❖ ❖ ❖

3	medium poblano chilies (about 9 ounces total)*
2	pounds small red-skinned potatoes, unpeeled, each cut into 6 wedges
6	medium tomatillos (about 7 ounces),** husked, cut into ½-inch pieces

1¼ cups chopped green onions
¼ cup chopped fresh cilantro

1 cup sour cream
3 tablespoons fresh lime juice
1¾ teaspoons ground cumin

Fresh cilantro sprigs

Char chilies over gas flame or in broiler until blackened on all sides. Enclose in paper bag; let stand 10 minutes. Peel and seed chilies. Cut chilies into ½-inch pieces. Transfer to large bowl.

Place potatoes on steamer rack set over boiling water in pot. Cover and steam until potatoes are just tender, about 10 minutes. Cool. Transfer to large bowl with roasted chilies. Mix in tomatillos, green onions and chopped cilantro.

Whisk sour cream, lime juice and cumin in small bowl to blend. Add to potato mixture and toss to coat. Season generously with salt and pepper. *(Can be prepared 6 hours ahead. Cover and refrigerate. Let stand at room temperature 30 minutes before serving.)*

Mound potato salad on platter. Garnish with cilantro sprigs.

*Fresh green chilies, often called pasillas; *available at Latin American markets and some supermarkets.*

**Green tomato-like vegetables with paper-thin husks; available at Latin American markets and some supermarkets.

4 TO 6 SERVINGS

Fennel Slaw with Black Pepper

◆ ◆ ◆

½ cup mayonnaise
¼ cup apple cider vinegar
2 tablespoons chopped fresh dill
1 tablespoon sugar
2 teaspoons black pepper
¾ teaspoon grated lemon peel
1½ pounds fresh fennel bulbs, trimmed, thinly sliced

Mix first 6 ingredients in large bowl. Add fennel and toss to coat. Season to taste with salt. *(Can be made 4 hours ahead. Cover and chill.)* Toss slaw again before serving.

4 SERVINGS

◆ ◆ ◆

Potato salad with a southwestern kick, which it gets (along with its name) from the addition of *poblano* chilies. It's a perfect partner for grilled flank steak, chicken or spice-rubbed fresh red snapper.

◆ ◆ ◆

Asian-Style Noodle Salad

◆ ◆ ◆

8	ounces spaghetti, broken in half
4	teaspoons oriental sesame oil
1	cup shredded carrot
½	red bell pepper, very thinly sliced
1	cup matchstick-size strips peeled jicama
1	cup (packed) spinach leaves (about 1 ounce), thinly sliced
3	tablespoons thick teriyaki marinade
3	tablespoons rice vinegar
2	tablespoons sugar
1	teaspoon minced garlic

Cook spaghetti in large pot of boiling salted water until just tender but still firm to bite. Drain; rinse with cold water and drain well. Place spaghetti in large bowl; add 1 teaspoon sesame oil and toss to blend. Add carrot, bell pepper, jicama and spinach to bowl.

Whisk next 4 ingredients and remaining 3 teaspoons sesame oil in small bowl to blend. Season dressing with salt and pepper. Add dressing to salad and toss to combine.

Divide salad among bowls and serve.

4 SERVINGS

The dressing here can also be used for Chinese chicken salad or as a basting sauce for grilled steaks or chops. Look for rice vinegar in the Asian foods section of the market.

◆ ◆ ◆

Green Bean and Mushroom Salad

◆ ◆ ◆

3	tablespoons balsamic vinegar
2	tablespoons fresh lemon juice
1	tablespoon olive oil
2	teaspoons water
½	pound green beans, trimmed, cut into 1½-inch pieces (about 2 cups)
2	fennel bulbs, quartered lengthwise, thinly sliced crosswise
4	ounces button mushrooms, trimmed, quartered (about 2 cups)
2	cups chopped fresh Italian parsley
3	tablespoons chopped fresh chives
2	teaspoons finely grated lemon peel

Whisk first 4 ingredients in medium bowl to blend. Season dressing to taste with salt and pepper.

Cook beans in large pot of boiling water until crisp-tender, 5 minutes. Drain. Transfer to bowl of ice water. Drain. Pat dry.

Place beans in large bowl. Add fennel, mushrooms, parsley, chives and lemon peel. Drizzle dressing over; toss. Season with salt and pepper. Cover and chill 30 minutes. Toss again and serve.

6 SERVINGS

Egg and Potato Salad

◆ ◆ ◆

2	pounds white potatoes, peeled, cut into 1-inch pieces
¼	cup low-fat mayonnaise
¼	cup nonfat milk
1	tablespoon Dijon mustard
1	tablespoon apple cider vinegar
3	large eggs, hard-boiled, peeled, coarsely chopped
1	cup thinly sliced celery
½	cup chopped green onions
⅓	cup pimiento-stuffed green olives, chopped
	Paprika

Place potatoes on steamer rack set in large pot over boiling water. Cover; steam potatoes until tender, about 10 minutes. Cool.

Whisk mayonnaise, milk, mustard and vinegar in large bowl to blend. Add potatoes, eggs, celery, green onions and olives; toss gently to blend. Season with salt and pepper. Sprinkle with paprika.

6 SERVINGS

THE TRUTH ABOUT EGGS

Eggs are easy to prepare, versatile, nutritious and cheap. Americans love them and eat a lot of them. But this wasn't always the case. Several decades ago, researchers discovered a link between elevated levels of blood cholesterol and heart disease. It was suspected that dietary cholesterol influenced the level of cholesterol in the blood. Consequently, we were told to limit our total cholesterol intake to less than 300 milligrams a day. Since one egg yolk has 213 milligrams of dietary cholesterol, eggs were made an extravagance.

More recent scientific research indicates that it might very well be saturated fat—more so than dietary cholesterol—that leads to high blood cholesterol. One large egg contains just 5 grams of total fat; of this fat, only 1.5 grams are saturated. (By way of comparison, a lean hamburger contains 5 grams of saturated fat.)

So eggs are back on the A-list now, especially when you consider that they are a good source of protein, iron and vitamins A, D and B$_{12}$, and have only 75 calories each. Which is not to say that you should fry a couple in half a stick of butter every morning, but don't hesitate to make them a part of your healthful, balanced diet.

◆ ◆ ◆

Honey Bran Muffins with Figs

◆ ◆ ◆

A light texture and a sweet honey flavor distinguish these breakfast treats. Lots of chopped dried figs make them irresistible.

◆ ◆ ◆

2½ cups all purpose flour
2   teaspoons baking soda
1½ teaspoons salt
2   cups toasted wheat bran (about 4 ounces)
¾   cup chopped dried figs
1   cup boiling water

½   cup (1 stick) unsalted butter, room temperature
1   cup sugar
½   cup honey
2   large eggs
2   cups buttermilk

Preheat oven to 400°F. Line 24 muffin cups with muffin papers. Stir all purpose flour, baking soda and salt in small bowl to blend. Combine toasted wheat bran and chopped figs in medium bowl; mix in 1 cup boiling water.

Beat unsalted butter in large bowl until creamy. Gradually beat

in sugar, then honey. Beat in eggs 1 at a time. Beat in buttermilk alternately with flour mixture, beginning with buttermilk, in 3 additions each. Stir in bran-fig mixture. Divide batter among muffin cups.

Bake bran muffins until tester inserted into center comes out clean, about 20 minutes. Turn muffins out onto racks and cool. *(Can be prepared 1 day ahead. Store in airtight container at room temperature.)* Serve muffins slightly warm or at room temperature.

MAKES 24

Lemon-Chive Biscuits

◆ ◆ ◆

3	cups plus 2 tablespoons cake flour
2½	cups plus 3 tablespoons bread flour
4½	tablespoons sugar
3½	tablespoons baking powder
1½	teaspoons salt
¾	cup (1½ sticks) unsalted butter, cut into small pieces, room temperature
¼	cup chopped fresh chives
¼	cup grated lemon peel
1	cup milk
4	large eggs
1	tablespoon water

Preheat oven to 400°F. Line heavy large baking sheet with parchment. Mix first 5 ingredients in large bowl. Using fingertips, rub butter into flour mixture until mixture resembles coarse meal. Stir in chives and lemon peel. Whisk milk and 3 eggs in medium bowl to blend. Add to flour mixture and stir just until blended.

Turn dough out onto lightly floured surface; knead gently just until dough comes together. Roll out dough to ½-inch thickness. Using 2½- to 3-inch round cookie cutter, cut dough into biscuits. Arrange biscuits on prepared baking sheet. Gather scraps into ball. Reroll to ½-inch thickness. Cut out additional biscuits. Arrange on prepared baking sheet. Whisk remaining 1 egg and 1 tablespoon water in small bowl to blend. Brush mixture over tops of biscuits.

Bake biscuits until golden, about 20 minutes. Transfer to rack and cool slightly. Serve warm or at room temperature. *(Can be prepared 1 day ahead. Store in airtight container at room temperature.)*

MAKES ABOUT 20

◆ ◆ ◆

Chopped chives and grated lemon peel accent these light biscuits. They can be served warm or made ahead and served at room temperature.

◆ ◆ ◆

Like classic Irish soda bread, these rolls are flecked with caraway seeds. Sweet golden raisins replace the more traditional dried currants with equally delicious results.

◆ ◆ ◆

Caraway and Raisin Soda Bread Rolls

◆ ◆ ◆

3½ cups cake flour
½ cup sugar
1½ teaspoons baking soda
¾ teaspoon salt
½ cup (1 stick) chilled unsalted butter, cut into ½-inch pieces
½ cup golden raisins
1 tablespoon caraway seeds
1 cup whole milk

Preheat oven to 400°F. Lightly butter baking sheet. Mix flour, sugar, baking soda and salt in large bowl. Add butter and rub in with fingertips until mixture resembles coarse meal. Mix in raisins and caraway seeds. Using fork, mix in milk, stirring until moist clumps form. Using floured hands and ⅓ cup dough for each, shape dough into 12 balls. Transfer to prepared baking sheet. Flatten into 2½-inch-diameter, 1-inch-thick rounds. Cut X in tops of rounds.

Bake rolls until golden brown and tester inserted into center comes out clean, 20 minutes. Serve warm or at room temperature.

MAKES 12

Featherweight Buttermilk Biscuits

◆ ◆ ◆

2	cups unbleached all purpose flour
1	tablespoon sugar
1	tablespoon cornstarch
2	teaspoons baking powder
½	teaspoon baking soda
½	teaspoon salt
¼	cup (½ stick) chilled unsalted butter, cut into ½-inch pieces
¾	cup chilled buttermilk

Preheat oven to 450°F. Sift first 6 ingredients into large bowl. Add butter and rub in with fingertips until mixture resembles coarse meal. Add buttermilk and stir until dough forms.

Turn dough out onto floured surface; knead until smooth, about 8 turns. Roll out dough to 1-inch thickness. Using 2-inch-diameter biscuit cutter or cookie cutter, cut out biscuits. Gather scraps; roll out to 1-inch thickness and cut out additional biscuits.

Transfer biscuits to large ungreased baking sheet. Bake until golden, about 12 minutes. Serve warm.

MAKES ABOUT 12

Onion and Poppy Seed Focaccia

◆ ◆ ◆

2	tablespoons olive oil
1	cup finely chopped onion
1	11-ounce package refrigerated French Loaf bread dough
¼	cup grated Parmesan cheese
2	teaspoons poppy seeds

Preheat oven to 400°F. Oil baking sheet. Heat 1 tablespoon oil in medium skillet over medium heat. Add onion and sauté until golden, about 7 minutes. Cool completely.

Place dough on floured surface. Fold dough in half. Using rolling pin, roll out dough to 10 x 8-inch rectangle. Transfer to prepared baking sheet. Drizzle 1 tablespoon oil over dough. Spread onion atop dough. Sprinkle with Parmesan and poppy seeds; sprinkle lightly with salt. Bake until bread is golden, about 18 minutes. Cut into pieces and serve warm or at room temperature.

6 SERVINGS

ALL ABOUT POPPY SEEDS

In this country, we're eating more poppy seeds now than ever. From 1976 to 1995, annual consumption rose from about 5.6 million pounds to almost 13.5 million pounds. And recently, the American Spice Trade Association ranked poppy seeds ninth on the list of our favorite spices, just behind oregano and ahead of white pepper. But in truth, we're just beginning to discover what home cooks in central and eastern Europe have known for generations: Poppy seeds, with their crunchy texture, nutty flavor and pleasing edge of bitterness, make a delicious addition to breads, muffins, cakes and pastries.

Poppies, it turns out, have been cultivated for food for more than five thousand years. Some scholars speculate that the Neolithic and Early Bronze Age peoples mixed the seeds of the flower with honey to form a rich paste—a sort of prehistoric candy bar. The poppy's history, though, has always been less about the seeds and more about opium, the narcotic, milky latex that fills the pods of *Papaver somniferum*, "the sleep-bearing poppy," before its seeds ever ripen. In reality, virtually all traces of opiates disappear by the time the seeds mature.

◆ ◆ ◆

QUICK BREADS

Yeast-leavened doughs require up to several hours to rise after they've been mixed and kneaded. Quick breads, by contrast, take advantage of other, faster rising methods: the carbon dioxide (gas) released by baking soda or baking powder, or the air incorporated into a batter or dough through beaten eggs.

You can put fresh-baked bread on your table in minutes, not hours, by preparing one of these quick breads.

- Biscuits: Mildly sweetened or slightly savory breads cut out from soda-leavened doughs, and generally served at breakfast.
- Loaves: Sweet or savory soda-leavened batters baked in loaf pans and served with breakfast or tea.
- Muffins: Individual breakfast breads made from soda-leavened batters baked in muffin cups.
- Popovers: Light, hollow breads lightened by milk and eggs, baked in special popover tins that transmit heat quickly. Traditionally served with roasted meats.
- Scones: Rich, sweetened, buttery quick breads cut from soda-leavened doughs and traditionally served at teatime.

◆ ◆ ◆

Orange Nut Bread

◆ ◆ ◆

1¾ cups all purpose flour
2½ teaspoons baking powder
¾   teaspoon salt
½   cup frozen orange juice concentrate, thawed
¼   cup water
1¼ cups sugar
5   tablespoons unsalted butter, room temperature
2   large eggs
½   cup chopped toasted almonds
1½ teaspoons grated orange peel

Preheat oven to 350°F. Lightly butter 8½ x 4½ x 2½-inch loaf pan; dust with flour. Sift flour, baking powder and salt into small bowl. Combine orange concentrate and ¼ cup water in another small bowl. Using electric mixer, beat sugar and butter in large bowl 1 minute. Beat in eggs 1 at a time. Beat in flour mixture alternately with orange concentrate mixture in 3 additions each. Mix in almonds and orange peel. Transfer batter to prepared pan.

Bake bread until tester inserted into center comes out clean, about 55 minutes. Cool bread in pan on rack 5 minutes. Turn out onto rack and cool completely. *(Can be made 2 days ahead. Wrap in plastic and store at room temperature.)*

MAKES 1 LOAF

Rosemary and Thyme Breadsticks

◆ ◆ ◆

2   cups bread flour
1¾ teaspoons salt
1½ teaspoons quick-rising yeast
1   tablespoon minced fresh rosemary
1   tablespoon minced fresh thyme
1   teaspoon honey
1   teaspoon olive oil (preferably extra-virgin)
¾   cup (about) warm water (120°F to 130°F)

Mix flour, salt and yeast in processor. Add rosemary, thyme, honey and oil. Gradually blend in enough water to bind dough together. Process until dough forms ball, about 30 seconds longer.

Turn dough out onto work surface. Knead until smooth and elastic, about 2 minutes. Lightly oil large bowl. Add dough; turn to coat with oil. Cover bowl with plastic wrap, then towel. Let dough rise in warm draft-free area until doubled, about 1 hour.

Punch down dough. Divide into 16 equal pieces. Roll each dough piece between palms and work surface into 12-inch-long by ½-inch-wide rope. Arrange ropes on 2 heavy large baking sheets, spacing 1 inch apart. Let rise uncovered in warm draft-free area until almost doubled, about 30 minutes.

Preheat oven to 325°F. Bake until breadsticks are very crisp and pale golden, about 40 minutes. Transfer breadsticks to racks and cool. *(Can be made 3 days ahead. Store airtight at room temperature.)*

MAKES 16

Grilled Bread with Catalan Butter

◆ ◆ ◆

6	tablespoons (¾ stick) butter, room temperature
2	hard-boiled large egg yolks
2	tablespoons finely chopped drained oil-packed sun-dried tomatoes, 1 tablespoon oil reserved
8	drained pimiento-stuffed green olives, finely chopped
4	canned anchovy fillets, drained, finely chopped
4	teaspoons drained capers
2	teaspoons chopped fresh rosemary
2	teaspoons fresh lemon juice
½	teaspoon dried crushed red pepper
2	cups hickory smoke chips, soaked in water 30 minutes, drained
12	½-inch-thick crusty country-style bread slices (each about 4 x 3 inches)

Anchovies, capers, olives and sun-dried tomatoes—typical Spanish ingredients—enhance the savory butter. It would also be good melted over grilled fish or chicken.

◆ ◆ ◆

Mash butter and yolks in medium bowl to form paste. Mix in sun-dried tomatoes, reserved 1 tablespoon oil and next 6 ingredients. Season with salt and pepper. *(Can be made 1 week ahead. Cover and freeze. Bring to room temperature before continuing.)*

Prepare barbecue (medium-high heat). Place smoke chips in 8 x 6-inch foil packet with open top. Set atop coals 5 minutes before grilling bread. Grill bread until toasted, 2 minutes per side.

Spread butter mixture over hot bread. Transfer to platter.

6 SERVINGS

·DESSERTS·

*Hazelnut Praline Cheesecake
(page 194) and Cappuccino
Chocolate Layer Cake (page 192).*

Black-Bottom Banana Cream Pie

◆ ◆ ◆

◆ ◆ ◆

A chocolate crust, chocolate ganache and banana cream filling make a stunning black-and-white pie. The crust, which combines cookie crumbs, melted chocolate and butter, becomes crisp when refrigerated.

◆ ◆ ◆

CRUST

½   cup (1 stick) unsalted butter

3   ounces semisweet chocolate, chopped

1½   cups chocolate wafer cookie crumbs (about 7 ounces)

CHOCOLATE GANACHE

½   cup whipping cream

1   tablespoon unsalted butter

4   ounces semisweet chocolate, chopped

½   teaspoon vanilla extract

4   ripe bananas (about 1½ pounds)
    Vanilla Pastry Cream (see recipe opposite)

    Vanilla Whipped Cream (see recipe opposite)

FOR CRUST: Butter 9-inch-diameter glass or ceramic pie dish. Stir butter and chocolate in heavy small saucepan over low heat until smooth. Remove from heat; mix in crumbs. Press onto bottom and up sides of prepared dish. Chill until firm, about 30 minutes.

FOR CHOCOLATE GANACHE: Heat cream and butter in medium saucepan over medium heat until mixture is hot (do not boil). Remove from heat. Add chocolate and vanilla. Whisk until smooth. Reserve 2 tablespoons chocolate ganache in small bowl at room temperature; pour remainder over crust. Chill crust until chocolate ganache is firm, about 30 minutes.

Thinly slice 3 bananas. Arrange banana slices over chocolate. Whisk Vanilla Pastry Cream until smooth. Spread pastry cream evenly over bananas. Drizzle reserved chocolate ganache over pastry cream. Draw toothpick through pastry cream and chocolate to marbleize. Refrigerate until pastry cream is set, about 3 hours. *(Can be made 1 day ahead. Cover and keep refrigerated.)*

Spoon Vanilla Whipped Cream around edges of pie, or spoon whipped cream into pastry bag fitted with large star tip and pipe cream around edges of pie. Slice remaining banana. Garnish pie with banana slices. Serve immediately.

8 SERVINGS

Vanilla Pastry Cream

1½ cups half and half
½   cup sugar
2   large eggs
1   large egg yolk
2   tablespoons all purpose flour
2   teaspoons vanilla extract

Bring half and half to simmer in heavy medium saucepan. Whisk sugar, eggs, egg yolk and flour in medium bowl to blend. Gradually whisk in hot half and half. Transfer to saucepan. Whisk over medium heat until mixture thickens and comes to boil, about 5 minutes. Boil 1 minute. Pour into medium bowl. Stir in vanilla. Press plastic onto surface of pastry cream. Cover; refrigerate until cold, about 4 hours. *(Can be made 1 day ahead. Keep chilled.)*

MAKES ABOUT 2 CUPS

Vanilla Whipped Cream

1   cup chilled whipping cream
1   tablespoon powdered sugar
½   teaspoon vanilla extract

Beat cream, powdered sugar and vanilla in large bowl until stiff peaks form. *(Can be made 4 hours ahead. Cover and chill.)*

MAKES ABOUT 1¾ CUPS

CLEVER GARNISHES

Want to add a quick, fancy flourish to a special dessert or drink? Try some of these insiders' tricks.

◆ Zest Spirals: Use a vegetable peeler to cut long, thin strips of citrus peel. Pierce the end of one strip with the tip of a wooden toothpick; then wind the strip around the toothpick, piercing the other end of the peel with the other tip to secure it. Repeat with the remaining zest strips and chill in a bowl of ice and water for at least one hour. Drain. Unfasten and slide out the toothpicks.

◆ Chocolate Curls: Let a large block of chocolate soften to room temperature. Draw a swivel-bladed vegetable peeler across a wide edge to make chocolate curls. Use immediately or chill in the refrigerator until serving time.

◆ Powdered Sugar Patterns: Place a doily or another paper pattern or a stencil atop a plain-surfaced cake, cheesecake or torte. Sift powdered sugar evenly over the surface. Carefully lift off the paper to leave a decorative design. (This works with cocoa powder, too.)

◆ ◆ ◆

Fresh Blackberry Pie

◆ ◆ ◆

It's easy to make leaves or other shapes to decorate the top of the pie using scraps of pastry dough. Simply roll out the extra dough and, using small cookie cutters or a sharp knife, cut out designs and arrange over the top crust before baking.

◆ ◆ ◆

CRUST

2   cups unbleached all purpose flour
1   teaspoon salt
⅔   cup chilled solid vegetable shortening, cut into pieces
¼   cup (about) ice water

FILLING

1   cup plus 1 tablespoon sugar
¼   cup unbleached all purpose flour
4   ½-pint baskets blackberries (about 5¼ cups)
2   tablespoons fresh lemon juice

     Whipped cream (optional)

FOR CRUST: Stir flour and salt in large bowl. Add shortening and rub in with fingertips until mixture resembles coarse meal. Using fork, gradually mix in enough water to bind dough together. Divide dough in half. Flatten each half into disk. Wrap in plastic and refrigerate until cold, at least 1 hour. *(Can be prepared 1 day ahead. Keep refrigerated. Soften slightly before rolling.)*

FOR FILLING: Position rack in bottom third of oven and preheat to 425°F. Stir 1 cup sugar and flour in large bowl to blend. Add berries and lemon juice and toss gently to combine.

Roll out 1 dough disk on lightly floured surface to 11- to 12-inch round. Transfer to 9-inch-diameter pie dish. Spoon filling into crust. Roll out remaining dough disk to 11- to 12-inch round; place dough over filling. Press crust edges together to seal. Fold overhang under. Crimp edge decoratively. Using small sharp knife, cut several slits in top crust for steam to escape. Sprinkle top crust with remaining 1 tablespoon sugar.

Bake pie 15 minutes. Reduce oven temperature to 350°F. Bake pie until crust is golden, about 45 minutes longer. Serve pie warm or at room temperature with whipped cream, if desired.

6 SERVINGS

Apricot and Cherry Crostata

◆ ◆ ◆

CRUST

1   cup all purpose flour
1   tablespoon sugar
¼   teaspoon salt
½   cup (1 stick) chilled unsalted butter, cut into ½-inch pieces
2   tablespoons (about) ice water

FILLING

7   large apricots (about 15 ounces)
1   cup halved pitted cherries (from about 10 ounces cherries)
⅓   cup sugar
½   cup apricot preserves

FOR CRUST: Blend flour, sugar and salt in processor. Add butter; cut in using on/off turns until mixture resembles coarse meal. Blend in water by tablespoonfuls until moist clumps form. Gather dough into ball; flatten into disk. Wrap in plastic; chill 30 minutes. *(Can be made 1 day ahead. Keep chilled.)*

Roll out dough between 2 sheets of plastic to 11-inch round. Remove top sheet of plastic from dough and invert dough onto 9-inch-diameter tart pan with removable bottom. Remove second sheet of plastic. Press dough onto bottom and up sides of tart pan. Fold excess dough in, forming double-thick sides. Pierce dough all over with fork. Freeze crust for 20 minutes.

Preheat oven to 375°F. Bake crust until set but still pale, piercing with fork if crust bubbles, about 25 minutes. Cool on rack. Maintain oven temperature.

FOR FILLING: Blanch apricots in pot of boiling water 1 minute. Transfer to bowl of ice water to cool. Drain. Peel, halve and pit apricots. Cut each apricot half into 3 wedges. Arrange, rounded side down, in cooled baked crust. Arrange pitted cherries over and around apricots. Sprinkle sugar over fruit.

Bake tart until apricots are tender, about 50 minutes. Transfer to rack. Stir apricot preserves in heavy small saucepan over low heat until melted. Strain. Brush strained liquid preserves over fruit in tart. Remove pan sides from tart. Place tart on platter. Serve slightly warm or at room temperature. *(Can be prepared 4 hours ahead. Let tart stand at room temperature.)*

6 SERVINGS

JAM VS. JELLY

Toast and jam. Peanut butter and jelly. As familiar as we are with these different fruit spreads and their uses, do we really know one from the other? Here's how to tell a jam from a jelly from a preserve.

◆ Jam: Finely chopped or pureed fruit that is combined with sugar and then boiled. This fruit mixture is never strained.

◆ Jelly: Pureed fruit boiled with water or juice, then strained to separate the fruit pieces. The juice jells as it cools, leaving a clear, brightly colored product that is smooth and tender in texture, but still firm enough to hold its shape when spooned out of the jar.

◆ Preserves: A chunkier version of jam, containing large pieces of fruit or even whole fruits. Pectin is often added to the recipe.

◆ ◆ ◆

Pear Croustade

◆ ◆ ◆

CRUST

1	cup all purpose flour
1½	tablespoons sugar
⅛	teaspoon salt
6	tablespoons (¾ stick) chilled unsalted butter, cut into ½-inch pieces
1	large egg yolk
1½	tablespoons ice water

FILLING

2	firm but ripe Bosc pears, peeled, quartered, cored, cut into ½-inch wedges
3	tablespoons sugar
1	tablespoon all purpose flour
1	tablespoon fresh lemon juice
¼	teaspoon ground allspice
1	large egg white, beaten to blend
1	tablespoon whipping cream

TOPPING

2	tablespoons all purpose flour
1	tablespoon sugar
1	tablespoon chilled unsalted butter, cut into ½-inch pieces

◆ ◆ ◆

No special pan is needed to make this free-form tart. The outer edge of the dough is folded over the pear filling, then pleated and pinched to seal.

FOR CRUST: Mix flour, sugar and salt in processor. Add butter. Using on/off turns, process until mixture resembles coarse meal. Transfer to large bowl. Mix egg yolk and 1½ tablespoons ice water in small bowl. Using fork, blend enough yolk mixture, ½ tablespoon at a time, into flour mixture to form moist clumps. Gather dough into ball; flatten into disk. Wrap in plastic. Chill until firm, about 1 hour. *(Can be prepared 1 day ahead. Keep refrigerated. Let soften slightly before rolling out.)*

Position rack in center of oven and preheat to 400°F. Roll out dough on floured parchment paper to 10-inch round. Transfer dough on parchment paper to large baking sheet.

FOR FILLING: Toss pears, sugar, flour, lemon juice and allspice in large bowl. Overlap pear slices atop dough, leaving 2-inch border. Fold dough over fruit, pleating loosely and pinching to seal any cracks. Brush dough with egg white. Drizzle cream over filling.

FOR TOPPING: Mix flour and sugar in small bowl. Rub in butter with fingertips until mixture forms small clumps. Sprinkle topping over filling. Bake tart until crust is golden and filling bubbles, about 40 minutes. Transfer baking sheet to rack; cool slightly, about 15 minutes. Slide metal spatula under crust to free from parchment. Using large tart pan bottom as aid, transfer tart to platter. Serve warm or at room temperature.

4 SERVINGS

Brown Sugar-Buttermilk Pie

◆ ◆ ◆

1	purchased frozen deep-dish 9-inch pie crust
1	cup (packed) golden brown sugar
3	tablespoons all purpose flour
3	large eggs
1	large egg yolk
1	teaspoon vanilla extract
1½	cups buttermilk
3	tablespoons unsalted butter, melted, cooled

Position rack in center of oven and preheat to 400°F. Thaw pie crust 10 minutes. Bake crust until pale golden, about 12 minutes. Transfer to rack and cool. Reduce oven temperature to 350°F.

Blend brown sugar and flour in processor. Add eggs, yolk and vanilla and process until blended. Add buttermilk and melted butter and process just to blend. Pour mixture into cooled crust.

Bake pie until filling puffs and is almost set but center still moves slightly when pan is shaken, about 45 minutes. Cool pie on rack to room temperature. Chill until cold, at least 2 hours and up to 1 day. Cut into wedges and serve.

6 TO 8 SERVINGS

ALL ABOUT BUTTERMILK

Myth: Buttermilk is fattening because it has lots of butter in it.

Truth: Buttermilk made from either nonfat or low-fat milk has only 88 to 120 calories per cup (and 10 to 25 milligrams of cholesterol).

What many people don't realize is that buttermilk originally got its name not from how much butter was mixed into it but from how it was made. Back in the days before commercial creameries, farmers used to churn butter only every two or three days. By that time, the cream they were using had soured. When the soured cream was churned and the butter floated to the top, a clean, slightly sour and tangy liquid was left at the bottom—buttermilk.

Today there are two types of buttermilk available: cultured and acidified. The cultured variety is made in a similar manner to yogurt, with a nonfat or one percent milk inoculated with a bacterial culture and fermented. Acidified buttermilk is made by using tartaric or citric acid, plus some additives, to sour the milk. Both kinds of buttermilk contain lactic acid (along with lecithin), which makes baked goods (like the brown sugar pie at left) extra-tender.

◆ ◆ ◆

Honey Apple Pie

♦ ♦ ♦

CRUST

2	cups all purpose flour
½	teaspoon sugar
½	teaspoon salt
¾	cup (1½ sticks) chilled unsalted butter, cut into ½-inch pieces
2	tablespoons chilled vegetable shortening, cut into ½-inch pieces
6	to 7 tablespoons chilled orange juice

FILLING

2	generous tablespoons coarsely chopped dried tart cherries
2	generous tablespoons finely chopped dried apricots
2	generous tablespoons finely chopped dried peaches
2	tablespoons orange juice
2½	pounds Golden Delicious apples, peeled, cored, thinly sliced
3½	tablespoons all purpose flour
½	teaspoon ground cinnamon
½	teaspoon ground cardamom
¼	cup honey
¼	cup (½ stick) unsalted butter, melted
1	tablespoon grated orange peel

FOR CRUST: Combine flour, sugar and salt in large bowl. Using fingertips, rub in butter until pieces range in size from rice grains to peas. Add shortening; rub in until pieces are size of small peas. Sprinkle 5 tablespoons juice over, tossing gently with fork to blend. Continue adding enough juice 1 tablespoon at a time to form moist clumps. Gather dough into ball; divide into 2 parts, 1 slightly larger than the other. Flatten into disks. Wrap in plastic; chill 1½ hours.

FOR FILLING: Mix cherries, apricots, peaches and orange juice in large bowl. Let stand 30 minutes. Mix in apples, flour, cinnamon and cardamom; then mix in honey, butter and orange peel.

Position rack in bottom third of oven and preheat to 425°F. Roll out larger dough disk on lightly floured surface to 13-inch round. Transfer dough to 9-inch-diameter glass pie dish. Trim overhang to ½ inch. Roll out second dough disk to 12-inch round. Using knife, cut dough into ½-inch-wide strips. Spoon filling into bottom crust. Arrange 6 pastry strips atop filling. Arrange 6 more strips at right angles, forming lattice. Fold under ends; crimp crust.

Bake pie 10 minutes. Reduce oven temperature to 350°F. Bake until apples are tender, 1 hour 10 minutes. Cool 1 hour on rack.

8 SERVINGS

For the crust, mix flour, sugar and salt. Using fingertips, rub the butter and then the shortening into the flour mixture to form small pea-size pieces.

Arrange 6 dough strips across pie, spacing evenly. Arrange remaining 6 dough strips diagonally across other strips to form lattice design. Fold under ends of lattice strips.

To crimp pie crust decoratively, pinch thumb and index finger of one hand together, forming *V*; then press knuckle of index finger on opposite hand into dough.

In this refreshing sweet, lemon juice flavors the tart's filling, while lime juice flavors the frozen cream that accompanies each serving.

♦ ♦ ♦

Lemon Tart with Frozen Lime Cream

♦ ♦ ♦

CRUST

1¼ cups all purpose flour

⅓ cup powdered sugar

¼ teaspoon salt

½ cup (1 stick) chilled unsalted butter, cut into ½-inch pieces

2 tablespoons (about) ice water

FILLING

¾ cup whipping cream

½ cup sugar

2 large eggs

6 tablespoons fresh lemon juice

2 tablespoons all purpose flour

2 teaspoons grated lemon peel

Frozen Lime Cream (see recipe opposite)

FOR CRUST: Blend flour, powdered sugar and salt in processor. Add butter pieces; process until coarse meal forms. Add ice water 1 tablespoon at a time; process until moist clumps form. Gather dough into ball; flatten into disk. Transfer to 9-inch-diameter tart pan with removable bottom. Press over bottom and up sides of pan. Pierce crust all over with fork. Freeze 30 minutes.

Preheat oven to 350°F. Bake crust until golden, approximately 25 minutes. Cool. Maintain oven temperature.

FOR FILLING: Whisk first 6 ingredients in medium bowl to blend. Pour into crust. Bake tart until filling is set, about 25 minutes. Cool tart completely in pan on rack. Chill until cold. *(Can be made 8 hours ahead. Keep chilled.)* Serve with Frozen Lime Cream.

8 SERVINGS

Frozen Lime Cream

PASTRY CREAM

¼   cup all purpose flour
¼   cup sugar
3   large egg yolks
1   cup whole milk
5   tablespoons fresh lime juice
2   teaspoons grated lime peel

MERINGUE

½   cup plus 2 tablespoons sugar
3   tablespoons water
4   large egg whites

FOR PASTRY CREAM: Whisk flour, sugar and yolks in medium bowl to blend. Bring milk to simmer in heavy medium saucepan. Gradually whisk hot milk into yolk mixture. Return mixture to same saucepan. Whisk over medium heat until pastry cream thickens and simmers, about 5 minutes. Remove from heat. Whisk in lime juice and peel. Cool pastry cream completely.

FOR MERINGUE: Combine ½ cup sugar and water in heavy small saucepan. Stir over low heat until sugar dissolves. Increase heat; boil until thermometer inserted into mixture registers 240°F, tilting pan to submerge bulb, about 5 minutes.

Meanwhile, beat egg whites in large bowl until soft peaks form. Add 2 tablespoons sugar; beat until stiff but not dry.

Slowly pour boiling syrup into beaten egg whites, beating until meringue is cool, about 5 minutes.

Whisk ¼ of meringue into pastry cream. Fold in remaining meringue. Freeze lime cream until firm, about 8 hours. *(Can be prepared up to 2 days ahead; keep frozen.)*

8 SERVINGS

THE MERINGUE MYSTERY

To hear it described, fluffy white meringue is one of the simplest of creations: a mixture of beaten egg whites and sugar, with a consistency ranging from soft to hard depending on how much sugar is added and how long the meringue cooks. Yet meringue can cause cooks endless frustration. Follow these guidelines to help you achieve meringue perfection.

◆ Separate the eggs carefully. Even a speck of yolk in the whites will keep them from beating properly.

◆ Use an unlined copper bowl or a little cream of tartar. A harmless chemical reaction strengthens the egg whites' air bubbles, for higher, fluffier whites.

◆ Add the sugar gradually. Beating it in one tablespoon at a time incorporates the sugar smoothly, avoiding grainy meringues.

◆ Cook carefully. Follow all heating or baking instructions to the letter. Overcooking causes beads of sugar to form on the surface of meringue. Undercooking causes it to weep.

◆ ◆ ◆

Fresh Fruit Compote with Hazelnut-Cinnamon Biscotti

◆ ◆ ◆

3	large oranges
1	16-ounce basket fresh strawberries, hulled, sliced
4	kiwis, peeled, sliced
2	tablespoons orange juice
2	tablespoons sugar
	Pinch of ground cinnamon
	Fresh mint sprigs (optional)
16	Hazelnut-Cinnamon Biscotti (see recipe below)

Cut peel and white pith from oranges. Working over large bowl to catch juices and using small sharp knife, cut between membranes to release segments. Add strawberries, kiwis, 2 tablespoons orange juice, sugar and cinnamon to bowl; toss to blend. Refrigerate at least 30 minutes and up to 3 hours.

Divide compote among 8 bowls. Garnish with mint sprigs, if desired. Serve with Hazelnut-Cinnamon Biscotti.

8 SERVINGS

◆ ◆ ◆

Oranges, strawberries and kiwis combine in this beautiful compote, which pairs well with crunchy, hazelnut-flavored biscotti. Make the compote up to three hours ahead and the cookies as much as three days ahead.

◆ ◆ ◆

Hazelnut-Cinnamon Biscotti

	Nonstick vegetable oil spray
3	cups all purpose flour
1	tablespoon baking powder
½	teaspoon salt
¼	teaspoon ground cinnamon
1	cup hazelnuts, toasted, husked (about 4 ounces)
¾	cup sugar
½	cup (1 stick) unsalted butter, room temperature
1	tablespoon grated orange peel
1	teaspoon vanilla extract
3	large eggs

Preheat oven to 350°F. Spray large baking sheet with vegetable oil spray. Mix flour, baking powder, salt and cinnamon in medium bowl; set aside. Coarsely chop hazelnuts in processor. Transfer to small bowl. Combine sugar and butter in processor; blend until fluffy. Add orange peel and vanilla extract and blend well. Add eggs 1 at a time, blending just until incorporated after each addition. Add flour mixture; mix using on/off turns until just blended. Mix in hazelnuts using on/off turns until just blended.

Turn dough out onto floured work surface. Divide dough in half. Roll each half into 9-inch-long, 2-inch-wide log. Space logs 3 inches apart on prepared sheet. Flatten each to 12-inch-long, 2½-inch-wide log. Bake until very light golden and firm, about 25 minutes. Cool on baking sheet 5 minutes. Maintain oven temperature.

Using metal spatula, transfer logs to work surface. Using serrated knife, cut logs diagonally into ¾-inch-wide slices. Place slices, cut side down, on large baking sheet. Bake 15 minutes. Turn biscotti over; bake until light golden and firm, about 15 minutes longer. Transfer biscotti to racks and cool. *(Can be made 3 days ahead. Store airtight at room temperature.)*

MAKES ABOUT 32

◆ ◆ ◆

LASAGNA DINNER FOR EIGHT

PLATTER OF CURED MEATS AND MARINATED VEGETABLES

MIXED-MUSHROOM LASAGNA WITH PARMESAN SAUCE (PAGE 124)

TOSSED SALAD WITH BALSAMIC VINAIGRETTE

BAROLO

FREST FRUIT COMPOTE WITH HAZELNUT-CINNAMON BISCOTTI (AT LEFT; PICTURED AT LEFT)

◆ ◆ ◆

Fruit Salad with Papaya-Mint Sauce

This fruit salad takes on Asian overtones with the inclusion of pineapple, papaya, lychees and toasted coconut. The pureed papaya sauce with mint is nice drizzled over the salad; it would also be good over vanilla ice cream or frozen yogurt.

◆ ◆ ◆

½	large pineapple, peeled, cored, cut into ½-inch pieces
1	medium papaya, peeled, seeded, cut into ½-inch pieces
½	large cantaloupe, peeled, seeded, cut into ½-inch pieces
1	11-ounce can peeled whole lychees in heavy syrup, drained, halved lengthwise
½	cup seedless red grapes, halved
½	cup seedless green grapes, halved
	Papaya-Mint Sauce (see recipe below)
¼	cup sweetened shredded or flaked coconut, toasted

Mix first 6 ingredients in large bowl. *(Can be made 4 hours ahead. Cover and refrigerate.)* Spoon fruit mixture into 6 small bowls or goblets. Drizzle sauce over fruit. Sprinkle with coconut.

6 SERVINGS

Papaya-Mint Sauce

1	large papaya, peeled, seeded, coarsely chopped (about 1½ cups)
5	tablespoons sugar
3	tablespoons fresh lime juice
1½	tablespoons coarsely chopped fresh mint

Puree all ingredients in processor until smooth. Transfer sauce to bowl. Cover and refrigerate until ready to use. *(Can be prepared 1 day ahead. Keep sauce refrigerated.)*

MAKES ABOUT 1 CUP

Poached Pears in Red Wine with Anise and Lemon

◆ ◆ ◆

1	750-ml bottle dry red wine
1	cup sugar
1	cup water
6	2 x 1-inch strips lemon peel (yellow part only)
1½	teaspoons aniseed

1   vanilla bean, split lengthwise

6   firm but ripe Bosc pears

1½ cups nonfat vanilla frozen yogurt

Combine first 5 ingredients in heavy large pot. Scrape in seeds from vanilla bean; add bean. Bring to boil, stirring until sugar dissolves. Remove from heat. Peel, halve and core pears. Add pears, rounded side down, to cooking liquid. Return cooking liquid to boil. Reduce heat to low, cover and simmer until pears are tender, basting occasionally with cooking liquid if necessary, about 25 minutes. Using slotted spoon, transfer pears to bowl.

Strain cooking liquid; discard solids. Return cooking liquid to pot. Boil until reduced to 1 cup, about 12 minutes. Pour syrup over pears. Chill until pears are cold, at least 3 hours or overnight. *(Can be prepared 1 day ahead. Keep refrigerated.)*

Scoop frozen yogurt onto plates. Place pears on plates. Spoon sauce over pears. Serve immediately.

6 SERVINGS

Baked Apples with Raisins

◆ ◆ ◆

6   7- to 8-ounce baking apples (such as Golden Delicious, Braeburn or Rome Beauty)

1¼ cups golden raisins

¾   cup (packed) golden brown sugar

1   cup apple juice

¼   cup (½ stick) unsalted butter

Preheat oven to 375°F. Using melon baller, scoop out stem, core and seeds of apples, leaving bottom intact. Using vegetable peeler, peel skin off top half of each apple. Arrange apples, cavity side up, in 13 x 9 x 2-inch glass baking dish.

Stir raisins and brown sugar in small bowl to blend. Pack about 2 tablespoons raisin mixture into cavity of each apple. Sprinkle any remaining raisin mixture into dish around apples. Pour juice over and around apples. Dot apples with butter.

Bake apples 15 minutes; baste with juices. Continue to bake until apples are slightly puffed and tender, basting every 10 minutes, about 1 hour 10 minutes. Remove baking dish from oven; let apples stand 10 minutes, basting occasionally.

Transfer apples to bowls. Spoon pan juices over and serve.

6 SERVINGS

Baked apples are something simple—and simply delicious—for dessert. These are filled with golden raisins and brown sugar. Gingersnaps are a fine go-with.

◆ ◆ ◆

Asian Pears with Ginger Syrup

♦ ♦ ♦

¼ cup water
1 tablespoon matchstick-size pieces peeled fresh ginger
1 cup pure maple syrup
2 tablespoons whiskey or brandy
1 teaspoon fresh lemon juice
1 teaspoon grated lemon peel
½ teaspoon ground nutmeg
4 7-ounce chilled Asian pears
2 tablespoons finely chopped crystallized ginger
1 tablespoon finely chopped fresh mint leaves

Combine ¼ cup water and fresh ginger in heavy medium saucepan. Cover; simmer until ginger is tender, about 5 minutes. Stir in syrup, whiskey, lemon juice, peel and nutmeg. Simmer 10 minutes to blend flavors, stirring occasionally.

Slice pears into rounds. Overlap 6 rounds on each plate. Drizzle sauce over. Top with crystallized ginger and mint.

6 SERVINGS

♦ ♦ ♦

Using frozen peaches and boysenberries in this crisp means that you can enjoy the flavors of summer all year round. Serve it with vanilla ice cream for a special treat.

Peach-Berry Upside-Down Crisp

♦ ♦ ♦

1 1-pound bag frozen unsweetened sliced peaches, thawed
2 cups (about 8 ounces) frozen unsweetened boysenberries
1 cup sugar
1 cup all purpose flour
½ cup old-fashioned oats
½ cup milk
1 teaspoon vanilla extract
½ cup (1 stick) unsalted butter, melted, cooled

Preheat oven to 400°F. Stir peaches, berries and ½ cup sugar in large bowl to blend. Let stand 15 minutes.

Meanwhile, stir flour, oats, milk, vanilla and remaining ½ cup sugar in medium bowl until blended. Mix in butter (batter will be thick). Spread in bottom of 8 x 8 x 2-inch glass baking dish.

Spoon fruit atop batter. Bake crisp until fruit is cooked through, about 45 minutes. Let stand 10 minutes. Serve warm.

6 TO 8 SERVINGS

Spiced Apple Napoleons with Pomegranate Caramel Sauce

◆ ◆ ◆

2   tablespoons plus ½ cup sugar
1   teaspoon ground cinnamon
2   sheets fresh phyllo pastry or frozen, thawed
3   tablespoons unsalted butter, melted

1½   cups plus 1 tablespoon water
½   teaspoon ground allspice
2¾   pounds tart green apples, peeled, cored, sliced ⅓ inch thick
¼   cup bourbon
1   tablespoon cornstarch

½   cup (packed) dark brown sugar
¼   cup pomegranate molasses*

Preheat oven to 375°F. Mix 2 tablespoons sugar and ¼ teaspoon cinnamon in small bowl. Place 1 phyllo sheet on work surface. Brush with half of melted butter. Sprinkle with half of cinnamon sugar. Top with second phyllo sheet. Brush with remaining butter. Sprinkle with remaining cinnamon sugar. Cut phyllo lengthwise in half; place 1 half atop other. Cut phyllo crosswise into 3 squares. Cut each square into 4 triangles for a total of 12 triangles. Place triangles on large baking sheet. Bake until deep golden, about 8 minutes. Cool on sheet.

Stir ½ cup sugar, ¾ teaspoon cinnamon, 1 cup water and allspice in large saucepan over low heat until sugar dissolves. Increase heat and bring to boil. Add apples; reduce heat and simmer until tender, stirring often, about 15 minutes. Mix in bourbon. Mix cornstarch and 1 tablespoon water in small bowl; add to apple mixture and stir until liquid thickens slightly and mixture boils, about 1 minute. Remove from heat. *(Phyllo triangles and apple mixture can be prepared 4 hours ahead. Cover separately. Let stand at room temperature. Rewarm apple mixture over low heat.)*

Stir ½ cup water and brown sugar in heavy small saucepan over medium heat until sugar dissolves. Increase heat and boil until slightly reduced, about 6 minutes. Add pomegranate molasses and boil until syrupy, about 4 minutes. Cool.

Place 1 phyllo triangle on each of 6 plates. Top with apple mixture. Top each with another phyllo triangle. Drizzle sauce over.

A thick pomegranate syrup, available at Middle Eastern markets and some supermarkets.

6 SERVINGS

Strawberry-topped Cheesecake with Graham Cracker Crust

♦ ♦ ♦

♦ ♦ ♦

Begin preparing this rich and creamy cheesecake a day ahead. After baking, it needs to be refrigerated overnight so that it sets up. You can top the cheesecake with the berries up to six hours before serving.

♦ ♦ ♦

CRUST

20   whole graham crackers (10 ounces total), broken

¾   cup (1½ sticks) chilled unsalted butter, diced

½   cup (packed) golden brown sugar

FILLING

4   8-ounce packages cream cheese, room temperature

1¾   cups sugar

3   tablespoons fresh lemon juice

2½   teaspoons vanilla extract
     Pinch of salt

3   tablespoons all purpose flour

5   large eggs

TOPPING

2   cups sour cream

3   tablespoons sugar

½   teaspoon vanilla extract

2   16-ounce baskets strawberries, hulled

1   18-ounce jar raspberry jelly

FOR CRUST: Position rack in center of oven and preheat to 350°F. Wrap foil around outside of 10-inch-diameter springform pan with 3-inch-high sides. Combine graham crackers, butter and sugar in processor. Using on/off turns, blend until crumbs begin to stick together. Press crumbs onto bottom and 2¾ inches up sides of springform pan. Bake crust 10 minutes. Transfer to rack and cool while preparing filling. Maintain oven temperature.

FOR FILLING: Beat cream cheese, sugar, lemon juice, vanilla and salt in large bowl until very smooth. Beat in flour. Add eggs and beat just until blended, stopping occasionally to scrape down sides of bowl. Pour batter into prepared crust.

Bake until outer 2-inch edge of cake is puffed and slightly cracked, center is just set and top is brown in spots, about 55 minutes. Transfer cake to rack. Cool 10 minutes. Maintain oven temperature.

FOR TOPPING: Whisk sour cream, sugar and vanilla in medium bowl to blend. Spoon topping over cake, spreading to edge of pan. Bake until topping is just set, about 5 minutes. Remove from oven. Run knife between crust and pan.

Cool hot cake in pan on rack. Refrigerate overnight.

Release pan sides from cheesecake. Arrange whole berries, points facing up, atop cheesecake; cover completely. Stir jelly in heavy small saucepan over medium-low heat until melted. Cool to barely lukewarm, about 5 minutes. Brush enough jelly over berries to glaze generously, allowing some to drip between berries. Reserve remaining glaze in saucepan. *(Cake and glaze can be prepared up to 6 hours ahead. Cover cake and refrigerate.)*

Rewarm remaining glaze until pourable. Cut cake into wedges. Serve, passing remaining glaze separately.

12 SERVINGS

Last year marked the first-ever poll of *Bon Appétit*'s readers. We learned, among other things, what you *do* and *do not* like to eat. Here are some of the results.

◆ Main Courses: Chicken was the overwhelming favorite, followed by beef, then pork. Salmon was the top fish; shrimp got the shellfish vote. Everyone's best-liked pasta dish? Not spaghetti but lasagna.

◆ Snacks: The most loved snack food was chips—potato, tortilla and otherwise—though popcorn got the top ranking when the question veered toward snacking in front of the TV. Favorite thing to eat standing over the kitchen sink: cookies.

◆ Desserts: Among the old-fashioned type, apple pie (à la mode, of course) got the highest honors, with crème brûlée topping the fancy dessert list. As for chocolate sweets, the ever-popular hot fudge sundae got top billing. Chocolate chip was the favored cookie, vanilla the ice cream everyone likes best. And what was the all-time favorite *Bon Appétit* recipe? The luscious cheesecake at left.

◆ ◆ ◆

The air trapped in beaten eggs causes the genoise batter to rise during baking; and warm eggs can be beaten to a fuller volume. Whisk the eggs with sugar and salt in a bowl set over simmering water until heated through and very foamy.

The warm egg mixture needs to be beaten on high speed until it triples in volume and falls off the beaters in a thick, heavy ribbon.

Carefully drizzle the melted lukewarm butter over the batter, folding it in with a spatula. Work gently to keep the batter from deflating.

Chocolate Genoise with Chocolate-Peppermint Ganache

◆ ◆ ◆

SYRUP

⅓ cup water

⅓ cup sugar

1½ tablespoons dark crème de cacao

½ teaspoon vanilla extract

GENOISE

Nonstick vegetable oil spray

¾ cup plus 2 tablespoons cake flour

⅓ cup plus 1 tablespoon unsweetened cocoa powder

¼ teaspoon baking soda

5 large eggs

1 large egg yolk

¾ cup plus 2 tablespoons sugar

¼ teaspoon salt

1½ teaspoons vanilla extract

4 tablespoons (½ stick) unsalted butter, melted, cooled

GANACHE

36 ounces semisweet chocolate, finely chopped

2½ cups whipping cream

¼ cup light corn syrup

1½ teaspoons peppermint extract

1 teaspoon vanilla extract

Chocolate curls (about 6 ounces)

FOR SYRUP: Stir water and sugar in small saucepan over low heat until sugar dissolves. Increase heat; boil. Remove from heat. Stir in crème de cacao and vanilla. *(Can be made 1 week ahead. Cover; chill.)*

FOR GENOISE: Preheat oven to 350°F. Butter and flour 9-inch-diameter springform pan with 2¾-inch-high sides; line bottom with parchment paper. Cover cake rack with paper towel; spray paper towel with nonstick vegetable oil spray.

Sift flour, cocoa powder and baking soda into small bowl 3 times. Combine eggs, egg yolk, sugar and salt in large stainless steel bowl. Set bowl over saucepan of simmering water (do not let bottom of bowl touch water). Whisk until mixture is just warm to touch (thermometer will register 110°F), about 2 minutes. Remove mixture from over water. Using electric mixer, beat until mixture triples in volume and falls in heavy ribbon when beaters are lifted, about 5 minutes. Beat in vanilla. Sift flour mixture over in 3 additions; fold gently to incorporate each time. Drizzle butter over and fold in (do not overmix or batter will deflate). Transfer batter to pan.

Bake cake until tester inserted into center comes out clean, about 40 minutes. Cut around pan sides; release sides. Turn cake out onto towel-covered rack; peel off parchment. Cool. *(Can be made 1 day ahead. Wrap; store at room temperature.)*

FOR GANACHE: Place chocolate in large bowl. Bring cream to boil in small saucepan. Pour cream over chocolate. Add corn syrup and peppermint and vanilla extracts; whisk until smooth. Cool to room temperature, stirring occasionally.

Transfer 3 cups ganache to medium bowl. Using electric mixer, beat until very thick and light colored, about 12 minutes.

Using long serrated knife, cut genoise horizontally into 3 layers. Place 1 cake layer on cardboard round or pan bottom. Brush cake with 3 tablespoons syrup. Spread ⅓ of whipped ganache over. Repeat 2 more times with remaining cake layers, syrup and whipped ganache. Spread 1 cup unwhipped ganache thinly over top and sides of cake. Refrigerate cake until coating sets, about 10 minutes.

If necessary, warm remaining unwhipped ganache until just pourable. Place cake on rack set over sheet of foil. Pour ganache over cake as glaze, spreading to cover top and sides smoothly. Chill until glaze begins to set, about 30 minutes. Place cake on platter. Press chocolate curls onto sides. Chill at least 2 hours.

10 TO 12 SERVINGS

♦ ♦ ♦

This impressive dessert features two classic components: the buttery sponge cake known as genoise and the rich chocolate frosting known as ganache. Making the genoise and sugar syrup ahead eliminates last-minute fuss. Any leftover ganache can be chilled, rolled into balls and presented as another classic treat: truffles.

♦ ♦ ♦

Carrot-Almond Cake with Whipped Cream

◆ ◆ ◆

Whipped cream sweetened with sugar and spiked with brandy would be the perfect partner for this moist, luscious cake. Leftovers are terrific with coffee the next day.

2	cups sifted all purpose flour
2	teaspoons baking soda
2	teaspoons ground cinnamon
1	teaspoon baking powder
1	teaspoon salt
4	large eggs
1	cup vegetable oil
1	cup sugar
1	cup (packed) golden brown sugar
2½	cups finely grated peeled carrots (about 1 pound)
1	8-ounce can crushed pineapple in syrup, drained
2	tablespoons brandy
2	teaspoons vanilla extract
2	teaspoons grated orange peel
1	cup sliced almonds, toasted
¾	cup dried currants
¼	cup orange marmalade
	Whipped cream

Preheat oven to 350°F. Butter and flour 12-cup Bundt pan. Whisk flour, baking soda, cinnamon, baking powder and salt in medium bowl to blend. Whisk eggs, oil and both sugars in large bowl to blend. Mix carrots, pineapple, brandy, vanilla and orange peel into egg mixture, then mix in almonds and currants. Add dry ingredients and stir just to blend. Transfer batter to prepared pan.

Bake cake until tester inserted near center comes out clean, approximately 1 hour. Cool cake in pan on rack 15 minutes. Turn cake out onto rack; cool completely.

Stir marmalade in heavy small saucepan over low heat until melted. Brush warm marmalade over cake. *(Can be made 1 day ahead. Cover with cake dome and store at room temperature.)* Serve cake with whipped cream.

10 TO 12 SERVINGS

Bourbon-Pecan Cake

◆ ◆ ◆

1   cup raisins
¾   cup bourbon

1   cup all purpose flour
½   teaspoon baking powder
½   teaspoon ground nutmeg
½   teaspoon salt
1   cup sugar
½   cup plus ¼ cup (1½ sticks) unsalted butter, room temperature
3   large eggs
¼   cup whole milk
¼   cup mild-flavored (light) molasses
¼   teaspoon baking soda
2   cups chopped pecans (about 8 ounces)

1½   cups powdered sugar, sifted
2   tablespoons (about) water

¼   cup sweetened shredded coconut, toasted
10   pecan halves, toasted

Soak raisins in bourbon in bowl 4 hours or overnight.

Preheat oven to 300°F. Butter and flour 12-cup Bundt pan. Drain raisins, reserving 7 tablespoons bourbon. Sift flour, baking powder, nutmeg and salt into medium bowl. Using electric mixer, beat sugar and ½ cup butter in large bowl to blend. Beat in eggs 1 at a time. Beat in dry ingredients. Mix milk, molasses and baking soda in small bowl to blend. Add milk mixture to batter, beating until fluffy. Stir in raisins, 4 tablespoons reserved bourbon and chopped pecans. Spoon batter into prepared pan.

Bake cake until tester inserted near center comes out clean, about 1 hour. Cool cake in pan on wire rack 30 minutes. Turn cake out onto rack and cool completely.

Cook remaining ¼ cup butter in heavy medium skillet over medium heat until beginning to brown, about 3 minutes. Pour into medium bowl. Let butter stand until cool but still liquid. Mix in 1 tablespoon bourbon. Gradually whisk in powdered sugar. Add enough water to form glaze that is smooth and pourable.

Brush cake with reserved 2 tablespoons bourbon. Drizzle glaze over cake. Sprinkle with toasted coconut. Garnish with pecans. *(Can be made 1 day ahead. Cover; let stand at room temperature.)*

8 TO 10 SERVINGS

LUCKY EATS

Cooks have long associated certain celebratory dishes with omens of good luck. The thimble traditionally hidden in a pecan cake similar to the one here may be traced back to all manner of tokens or coins hidden in the steamed plum puddings served at British Christmas feasts. Whoever discovered one of the charms was deemed to have a bright omen for the coming year (as long as the discovery didn't break a tooth!).

Sweets aren't the only lucky foods. Hoppin' John, the Southern dish of black-eyed peas and rice, is always served on New Year's Day to usher in good fortune. The Chinese believe that eating long, hand-pulled noodles brings the promise of a long life. And who can forget Western culture's obsession with the wishbone?

Not all lucky-food customs, though, come to us from olden times. One story suggests that during the Great Depression of the 1930s, for example, a baker in Los Angeles's Chinatown came up with an ingenious idea for cheering up the hordes of out-of-work people he saw outside his shop. He took thin cookies hot from the oven, placed strips of paper with printed sayings on top, and folded the sides of the cookies up. The result: fortune cookies.

◆ ◆ ◆

Cappuccino Chocolate Layer Cake

Cups of steaming cappuccino inspired this chocolate cake accented with cinnamon and coffee. It's a perfect dessert for any birthday celebration. The velvety cake is easily cut into layers, each of which will hold a generous amount of frosting.

COFFEE SYRUP

6	tablespoons water
3	tablespoons sugar
1	tablespoon instant coffee powder

CAKE

4	ounces unsweetened chocolate, chopped
2	cups all purpose flour
1½	teaspoons baking powder
1	teaspoon ground cinnamon
¼	teaspoon salt
2	teaspoons instant coffee powder
1½	cups whole milk
2	cups sugar
½	cup (1 stick) unsalted butter, room temperature
2	large eggs
2	teaspoons vanilla extract

Fudge Frosting (see recipe opposite)

FOR COFFEE SYRUP: Combine all ingredients in small saucepan. Stir over low heat until sugar and coffee dissolve. Let cool. *(Can be made 2 days ahead. Cover and refrigerate.)*

FOR CAKE: Position rack in center of oven; preheat to 350°F. Butter two 9-inch-diameter cake pans with 2-inch-high sides. Line bottoms with waxed paper; butter paper. Dust with flour. Stir chocolate in top of double boiler set over simmering water until melted. Remove chocolate from over water.

Sift flour, baking powder, cinnamon and salt into medium bowl. Stir coffee powder into milk in another medium bowl until dissolved. Using electric mixer, beat sugar and butter in large bowl until well blended. Beat in eggs 1 at a time. Mix in melted chocolate and vanilla. Add dry ingredients alternately with milk mixture in 3 additions. Divide batter between prepared pans.

Bake cakes until tester inserted into center comes out clean, about 35 minutes. Cool cakes in pans on racks 10 minutes. Cut around pan sides. Turn cakes out onto wire racks and cool completely. Carefully peel off waxed paper.

Cut each cake horizontally in half. Using bottom of tart pan as aid, transfer 1 cake layer, cut side up, to platter. Brush cake layer

with 2 tablespoons syrup. Spread ¾ cup frosting over cake layer. Repeat layering 2 times, using 1 cake layer, 2 tablespoons syrup and ¾ cup frosting for each layer. Top with fourth cake layer, cut side down. Spread remaining frosting over cake. *(Can be made 1 day ahead. Cover and let stand at room temperature.)*

12 SERVINGS

Fudge Frosting

¾ cup (1½ sticks) unsalted butter

¾ cup sugar

¾ cup half and half

4 teaspoons instant coffee powder

6 ounces unsweetened chocolate, chopped

4 ounces semisweet chocolate, chopped

1 teaspoon vanilla extract

2½ cups powdered sugar

4 teaspoons ground cinnamon

Combine butter, ¾ cup sugar, half and half and coffee powder in large saucepan. Stir over medium heat until sugar and coffee powder dissolve and mixture simmers. Remove from heat. Add both chocolates; whisk until smooth. Whisk in vanilla. Pour chocolate mixture into large bowl. Sift in powdered sugar and cinnamon; whisk to blend. Press plastic onto surface of frosting. Chill just until firm enough to spread, stirring occasionally, about 1½ hours.

MAKES ABOUT 4 CUPS

♦ ♦ ♦

BIRTHDAY DINNER FOR SIX

SPINACH SALAD

BEEF WITH MARROW SAUCE AND GLAZED ONIONS
(PAGE 46)

ROASTED POTATO WEDGES

ASPARAGUS TIPS

CABERNET SAUVIGNON

CAPPUCCINO CHOCOLATE LAYER CAKE
(AT LEFT; PICTURED AT LEFT)

♦ ♦ ♦

Hazelnut Praline Cheesecake

◆ ◆ ◆

PRALINE

¾ cup sugar

¼ cup water

1 cup hazelnuts (about 5 ounces), toasted, husked

CRUST

1¼ cups cake flour

10 tablespoons chilled unsalted butter, cut into ½-inch pieces

¼ cup (packed) golden brown sugar

FILLING

4 8-ounce packages cream cheese, room temperature

1 cup sugar

2 tablespoons all purpose flour

2 tablespoons whipping cream

1 teaspoon vanilla extract

4 large eggs

◆ ◆ ◆

Crunchy hazelnut praline (which can be made up to a month ahead and happens to be delicious as a candy, too) adds a touch of sophistication to this rich cheesecake. Begin preparing it at least one day ahead.

◆ ◆ ◆

FOR PRALINE: Lightly oil baking sheet. Combine sugar and ¼ cup water in heavy medium saucepan. Stir over low heat until sugar dissolves. Increase heat; boil without stirring until syrup turns golden, occasionally brushing down sides of pan with wet pastry brush and swirling pan, 8 minutes. Add hazelnuts; stir until coated, 1 minute. Pour hot praline onto baking sheet. Cool until praline hardens. Break into pieces. Transfer to resealable plastic bag. Using rolling pin, coarsely crush praline. *(Can be made 1 month ahead. Store in airtight container and freeze.)*

FOR CRUST: Position rack in center of oven; preheat to 350°F. Butter 9-inch-diameter springform pan with 2¾-inch-high sides. Mix flour, butter and sugar in processor until moist clumps form. Press onto bottom of pan. Bake until crust is golden, about 25 minutes. Cool. Wrap outside of pan with double layer of foil.

FOR FILLING: Reserve ½ cup praline for garnish. Grind remaining praline to powder in processor. Beat cream cheese and sugar in large bowl until smooth. Beat in flour, then cream and vanilla. Beat in eggs 1 at a time. Fold in praline powder.

Transfer filling to crust. Place springform pan in roasting pan. Pour enough hot water into roasting pan to come halfway up sides of springform pan. Bake until center is just set, about 1 hour 20 minutes.

Transfer to rack. Run knife around sides of cake to loosen.

Cool completely. Remove foil from pan. Chill cake overnight. *(Can be made 3 days ahead. Cover; keep chilled.)*

Release pan sides. Mound crushed praline atop cake.

12 SERVINGS

Apple-Ginger Upside-Down Cake

◆ ◆ ◆

TOPPING

¼ cup (½ stick) unsalted butter

⅔ cup (packed) golden brown sugar

½ teaspoon ground ginger

4 large Granny Smith apples (about 28 ounces), peeled, quartered, cored, cut into ½-inch-thick wedges

3 tablespoons minced crystallized ginger

CAKE

⅓ cup minced crystallized ginger

4 tablespoons plus 1¼ cups all purpose flour

1 teaspoon baking powder

¼ teaspoon salt

1 cup (packed) golden brown sugar

6 tablespoons (¾ stick) unsalted butter, room temperature

2 large eggs

½ teaspoon vanilla extract

¼ cup whole milk

FOR TOPPING: Position rack in center of oven and preheat to 350°F. Butter 9-inch-diameter cake pan with 2-inch-high sides. Melt butter in small saucepan over medium heat. Add sugar and cook until mixture bubbles, about 3 minutes. Remove from heat. Stir in ground ginger. Pour mixture into prepared pan, spreading with spatula to distribute evenly. Tightly overlap apples atop sugar mixture, making 2 layers of apples. Sprinkle crystallized ginger atop apples.

FOR CAKE: Mix crystallized ginger with 1 tablespoon flour in small bowl. Sift 1¼ cups plus 3 tablespoons flour, baking powder and salt into medium bowl. Using electric mixer, beat brown sugar and butter in large bowl until light and creamy. Beat in eggs 1 at a time. Beat in vanilla. Mix in dry ingredients alternately with milk. Stir in ginger. Spoon batter atop apples. Bake until tester comes out clean, about 1 hour. Cool in pan on rack 15 minutes.

Run knife around edges of pan. Invert cake onto platter.

8 TO 10 SERVINGS

This old-fashioned upside-down cake has been updated with apples and crystallized ginger. Whipped cream flavored with ground ginger and sugar is a nice complement.

◆ ◆ ◆

Lemon Mousse with Boysenberry Puree

◆ ◆ ◆

◆ ◆ ◆

The foundation of this recipe is a lemon curd that can be served on its own with, say, scones or toasted brioches, or partnered with fruit. In this layered indulgence (pictured opposite with a Tangerine Soufflé, page 202), some of the curd is combined with whipped cream to make the mousse, and some is used on its own. When covering the lemon curd, make sure that the plastic wrap touches the surface to keep a "skin" from forming on the top.

◆ ◆ ◆

¾   cup plus 6 tablespoons sugar

4   large eggs

4   large egg yolks

1   cup fresh lemon juice

½   cup plus 2 tablespoons (1¼ sticks) unsalted butter

¾   cup frozen boysenberries, thawed, drained

1¾   cups chilled whipping cream

Fresh boysenberries (optional)

Whisk ¾ cup plus 2 tablespoons sugar, eggs and yolks in medium stainless steel bowl to blend. Bring lemon juice and butter to boil in heavy small saucepan. Gradually whisk hot lemon mixture into egg mixture. Set bowl over saucepan of simmering water (do not allow bottom of bowl to touch water). Stir until beginning to thicken and thermometer inserted into mixture registers 160°F, about 4 minutes. Transfer curd to small bowl. Press plastic wrap onto surface of curd; refrigerate until cold.

Puree thawed boysenberries and 4 tablespoons sugar in blender. Strain into medium bowl to remove seeds. *(Curd and puree can be made 1 day ahead. Cover puree; chill curd and puree.)*

Using electric mixer, beat cream in large bowl until soft peaks form. Transfer ¾ cup whipped cream to small bowl and reserve. Fold 1 cup curd into whipped cream to make mousse; reserve remaining curd. Spoon mousse into pastry bag fitted with large plain tip.

Spoon 1 tablespoon berry puree into bottom of each of 6 Champagne flutes or 6- to 8-ounce wineglasses. Pipe ¾-inch-thick layer of mousse over puree and top with generous 1 tablespoon reserved curd. Repeat layering with mousse and curd. Top with reserved whipped cream. *(Can be made 8 hours ahead. Cover and refrigerate.)* Garnish with fresh boysenberries, if desired.

6 SERVINGS

Strawberry Soufflé with
Sliced Strawberries

◆ ◆ ◆

Like a typical soufflé, this recipe is light and airy. Unlike most other soufflés, this version has no egg yolks, which makes it very low in calories, fat and cholesterol.

◆ ◆ ◆

	Nonstick vegetable oil spray
2	12-ounce baskets strawberries, hulled
7	tablespoons sugar
1	tablespoon cornstarch
¾	teaspoon grated orange peel
4	large egg whites

Preheat oven to 400°F. Spray 6-cup soufflé dish with vegetable oil spray. Coarsely puree half of berries, 3 tablespoons sugar and cornstarch in processor. Transfer to small saucepan. Stir over medium heat until mixture boils and thickens, about 3 minutes. Whisk in grated orange peel. Cool puree completely.

Slice remaining berries. Transfer berries to medium bowl. Add 1 tablespoon sugar; toss to blend. Beat egg whites in large bowl until soft peaks form. Gradually add 3 tablespoons sugar; beat until stiff but not dry. Fold puree into whites in 3 additions. Transfer to prepared dish. Bake until soufflé is puffed and golden, about 18 minutes. Serve immediately with sliced berries.

8 SERVINGS

Warm Citrus Gratin

◆ ◆ ◆

4	lemons
1½	cups whole milk
⅓	cup sugar
2	tablespoons all purpose flour
1	teaspoon cornstarch
5	large egg yolks
1	tablespoon fresh lemon juice
1	tablespoon unsalted butter, room temperature
½	teaspoon vanilla extract
½	cup mascarpone cheese*
3	navel oranges, peel and white pith removed
6	teaspoons powdered sugar

Using vegetable peeler, remove peel (yellow part only) from lemons in long strips. Pour milk into heavy 1-quart saucepan. Bring to simmer. Remove from heat. Add lemon peel. Cover and let stand 1 hour. Strain milk; discard peel. Return to pan.

Mix ⅓ cup sugar, flour and cornstarch in cup. Using electric mixer, beat yolks in large bowl until light. Add sugar mixture to yolks; beat until light, about 1 minute.

Bring milk to simmer again. Gradually whisk hot milk into yolk mixture. Return mixture to saucepan. Stir over low heat until custard thickens and bubbles. Remove from heat. Whisk in lemon juice, butter and vanilla extract, then mascarpone cheese. Cool slightly.

Using small sharp knife and working over medium bowl, cut oranges between membranes to release segments. *(Custard and orange segments can be prepared 1 day ahead. Cover separately and refrigerate. Rewarm custard over medium-low heat.)*

Preheat broiler. Divide warm custard among six 1-cup broiler-proof gratin dishes or custard cups. Arrange orange segments atop custard. Gently press on segments to submerge slightly. Sprinkle 1 teaspoon powdered sugar over each. Place on baking sheet. Broil until sugar browns, rotating gratins for even broiling if necessary and watching closely, about 3 minutes. Transfer dishes to plates and serve.

*Available at Italian markets and many supermarkets.

6 SERVINGS

◆ ◆ ◆

Sprinkling this creamy custard with powdered sugar and then placing the dessert under the broiler gives it a delicate crust. Serve some crisp cookies alongside, if you like.

◆ ◆ ◆

THE MOUSSE...

When you creatively combine cream or milk, eggs, sugar, gelatin and flavorings, so many different kinds of desserts can result that it's sometimes hard to tell one from another. Use these terms as a guide.

◆ Bavarian Cream: A molded dessert made by combining a pourable, egg-enriched custard with whipped cream and gelatin.

◆ Blancmange: A molded dessert of gelatin and whipped cream, traditionally flavored with a sweetened "milk" made with blanched, crushed almonds.

◆ Crème Brûlée: Literally "burned cream," this thick, smooth custard dessert is chilled in heatproof dishes. Shortly before serving, it's covered with a layer of sugar that is quickly caramelized to a deep-brown hue and glassy texture beneath a broiler.

◆ Custard: Any rich dessert based on egg yolks, sugar and milk or cream is technically a custard, including crème brûlée, flan and *pots de crème*. Traditionally, the term applies to pouring custard, a thick dessert sauce, and to baked egg custards, which have a firmer texture resulting from longer cooking and the inclusion of egg whites.

Chocolate Soufflés with White Chocolate Cream

◆ ◆ ◆

3	tablespoons water
1	tablespoon instant espresso powder or instant coffee powder
5	ounces semisweet chocolate, chopped
1	tablespoon brandy
3	large egg yolks
4	large egg whites
2½	tablespoons sugar

Powdered sugar
White Chocolate Cream (see recipe below)

Butter four ⅔-cup soufflé dishes; coat with sugar. Stir 3 tablespoons water and instant espresso powder in heavy small saucepan until espresso powder dissolves. Add chocolate and brandy. Stir over low heat until mixture is smooth. Remove from heat. Whisk in yolks. Cool to room temperature.

Beat 4 egg whites in large bowl until foamy. Gradually add 2½ tablespoons sugar and beat until medium-firm peaks form. Fold chocolate mixture into whites. Divide among soufflé dishes. Place soufflés on baking sheet. *(Can be made 2 hours ahead. Let stand uncovered at room temperature.)*

Preheat oven to 400°F. Bake soufflés until puffed but still moist in center, about 14 minutes. Dust soufflés with powdered sugar. Serve immediately, passing White Chocolate Cream separately.

4 SERVINGS

White Chocolate Cream

2	ounces good-quality white chocolate (such as Lindt or Baker's), chopped
½	cup chilled whipping cream

Stir chocolate in top of double boiler set over simmering water until smooth. Remove from water. Cool to room temperature. Beat cream in medium bowl until firm peaks form. Stir half of cream into cooled chocolate; fold in remaining cream. *(Can be made 4 hours ahead. Cover and refrigerate.)*

MAKES ABOUT 1 CUP

Caramel Pots de Crème

◆ ◆ ◆

1¼ cups sugar

¼ cup water

1¾ cups whipping cream

½ cup whole milk

6 large egg yolks

Position rack in center of oven and preheat to 325°F. Place six ⅔-cup soufflé dishes or ¾-cup custard cups in large roasting pan. Combine sugar and water in heavy large saucepan. Stir over low heat until sugar dissolves. Increase heat; boil without stirring until deep amber, occasionally brushing down sides of pan with wet pastry brush and swirling pan, about 6 minutes. Gradually whisk in 1½ cups whipping cream and milk (mixture will bubble vigorously). Stir until caramel dissolves, about 2 minutes.

Beat yolks in large bowl until foamy. Gradually whisk in warm caramel. Strain into 4-cup glass measuring cup. Divide among dishes. Pour enough hot water into pan to come halfway up sides of dishes. Cover pan with foil. Bake until custard is just set at edges but still moves in center when shaken gently, about 1 hour. Remove from water; cool on rack. Chill until cold, at least 2 hours. *(Can be made 2 days ahead. Cover; keep chilled.)*

Beat ¼ cup cream in small bowl until soft peaks form. Spoon cream into pastry bag fitted with large star tip. Pipe 1 rosette in center of each custard. Serve chilled.

6 SERVINGS

...AND THE FOOL

◆ Flan: The Spanish-language term for an egg custard dessert baked in a dish and usually served unmolded. If the mold is first lined with a caramelized sugar syrup before baking, the caramel partly melts, forming a sauce for the un-molded dessert; the result becomes the French *crème caramel*.

◆ Fool: A popular English dessert consisting of pureed, sweetened fruit folded into whipped cream, this probably derives its name from the French *fouler*, "to crush."

◆ Mousse: From the French for "froth" or "foam," *mousse* describes a sweet base, such as melted chocolate, lightened with beaten egg whites and chilled.

◆ Pots de Crème: Baked custards that are only lightly set to a thick, creamy consistency.

◆ Pudding: In Britain, the term gener-ally refers to dessert and more specifically to a heavy-textured, starchy pudding steamed in a mold. Outside Britain, puddings cover a range of creamy, spoonable desserts, including those made with rice and tapioca.

◆ Whip: Similar to a fool, this even lighter dessert adds beaten egg whites to the mixture of whipped cream and pureed fruit.

◆ ◆ ◆

Strawberry and Rhubarb Parfaits

◆ ◆ ◆

4	cups 1½-inch pieces rhubarb
½	cup water
¼	cup plus 2 tablespoons sugar
1	vanilla bean, split lengthwise
1	16-ounce basket fresh strawberries, hulled, thickly sliced
1	32-ounce container plain low-fat yogurt
2½	teaspoons vanilla extract
8	teaspoons (packed) golden brown sugar

Combine rhubarb, ½ cup water and sugar in heavy large saucepan. Scrape in seeds from vanilla bean; add bean. Cook over medium heat until rhubarb is almost tender, stirring occasionally, about 7 minutes. Add strawberries and cook 3 minutes. Transfer to bowl; discard bean. Refrigerate until cold, about 4 hours.

Mix yogurt and vanilla extract in medium bowl. In each of 8 wineglasses or goblets, layer scant ¼ cup yogurt mixture, ½ teaspoon golden brown sugar and ¼ cup strawberry-rhubarb mixture. Repeat layering. *(Can be prepared 4 hours ahead. Cover and chill.)*

8 SERVINGS

Tangerine Soufflés

◆ ◆ ◆

2	cups orange juice
1½	cups plus 2 tablespoons sugar
1	pound unpeeled tangerines (about 5 small), quartered, seeded
2	cups chilled whipping cream
2	tablespoons Grand Marnier
6	large egg whites

Bring orange juice, 1 cup sugar and tangerines to boil in heavy medium saucepan over medium-high heat, stirring until sugar dissolves. Cover pan, reduce heat to medium-low and simmer until tangerines are very tender, about 35 minutes. Strain mixture through sieve set over medium bowl, pressing firmly on fruit. Transfer fruit to processor; puree until tangerine peel is finely chopped. Return puree to saucepan; mix in ½ cup strained syrup, reserving remaining syrup for another use. *(Puree can be prepared 1 day ahead. Cover and refrigerate.)*

◆ ◆ ◆

What's the secret to a good soufflé? Beating the egg whites with the sugar until they are stiff and still very shiny, then folding them into the flavor base carefully in two or three additions so that the whites do not deflate. This dessert has an intense tangerine flavor, which comes from using the entire fruit, except for its seeds. Any leftover tangerine syrup can be added to sparkling wine to make a mimosa with a twist.

◆ ◆ ◆

Preheat oven to 400°F. Beat cream, Grand Marnier and 2 tablespoons sugar in large bowl until stiff peaks form; refrigerate. Butter ten ⅔-cup soufflé dishes or ramekins; dust with sugar and arrange on baking sheet. Stir puree over low heat until warm.

Beat egg whites in another large bowl until soft peaks form. Beat in ½ cup sugar, 1 tablespoon at a time, until egg whites are stiff and glossy. Fold ¼ of whites into warm tangerine puree in saucepan. Fold tangerine mixture into remaining whites in bowl. Divide soufflé mixture among prepared dishes on sheet. Bake until puffed and brown, about 16 minutes. Serve soufflés with whipped cream.

10 SERVINGS

Bread and Butter Pudding

◆ ◆ ◆

1½ cups whole milk
1½ cups whipping cream
1 vanilla bean, split lengthwise
8 large egg yolks
¾ cup plus 2 tablespoons sugar

¼ cup (½ stick) unsalted butter, room temperature
1 1-pound loaf white bread, slices cut ½ inch thick, crusts trimmed
2 tablespoons golden raisins
2 tablespoons brown raisins

Combine milk and whipping cream in heavy large saucepan. Scrape in seeds from vanilla bean; add bean. Bring milk mixture to simmer. Whisk egg yolks and ¾ cup sugar in large bowl to blend. Gradually whisk hot milk mixture into yolk mixture. Set aside.

Butter 9 x 9 x 2-inch glass baking dish. Spread ¼ cup butter over both sides of bread slices. Arrange ⅓ of bread slices in single layer over bottom of prepared dish, trimming to fit. Sprinkle half of golden raisins and half of brown raisins over bread. Cover with another single layer of bread. Sprinkle remaining raisins over. Layer with remaining bread. Discard vanilla bean from custard; pour over bread. Let stand until some custard is absorbed, 20 minutes.

Position rack in center of oven and preheat to 350°F. Bake pudding until custard thickens and begins to set, about 20 minutes.

Preheat broiler. Sprinkle remaining 2 tablespoons sugar over pudding. Broil until sugar browns, rotating dish for even browning, 2 minutes. Let cool slightly. Serve warm.

8 SERVINGS

Making bread pudding is a good way to use up day-old bread. This is a sensational version of the classic English dessert, with cream, whole milk and egg yolks making it ultra-rich.

Warm Walnut Brownie Pudding

♦ ♦ ♦

SYRUP
¾ cup (packed) dark brown sugar
¼ cup lightly packed unsweetened cocoa powder (preferably Dutch-process)
5 teaspoons instant espresso powder
  Pinch of salt
1⅔ cups warm water
1½ tablespoons vanilla extract

BROWNIE
1 cup all purpose flour
¾ cup sugar
¼ cup lightly packed unsweetened cocoa powder (preferably Dutch-process)
2 teaspoons baking powder
½ teaspoon salt
½ cup buttermilk
¼ cup (½ stick) unsalted butter, melted
¾ teaspoon vanilla extract
1 cup chopped walnuts, toasted

  Whipped cream

♦ ♦ ♦

Brownies are baked with a chocolate syrup that sinks to the bottom and thickens into a fudgy sauce, creating a luscious layering of textures.

FOR SYRUP: Combine first 4 ingredients in small saucepan. Gradually whisk in 1⅔ cups warm water and vanilla. Bring to simmer over low heat, whisking often. *(Can be made 2 days ahead. Cover and refrigerate. Rewarm over low heat before continuing.)*

FOR BROWNIE: Preheat oven to 325°F. Grease 8 x 8 x 2-inch baking pan with shortening. Whisk first 5 ingredients in large bowl to blend. Mix in buttermilk, butter and vanilla, then walnuts (batter will be thick). Spread in prepared pan. Pour syrup over brownie.

Bake brownie until sauce bubbles around sides and brownie layer has risen almost to top of pan and feels firm to touch, about 40 minutes. Transfer to rack and cool 10 minutes.

Cut dessert into squares. Serve warm with whipped cream.

6 TO 8 SERVINGS

Vanilla-Lime Flan

❖ ❖ ❖

1⅓ cups plus ½ cup sugar

½ cup water

4 teaspoons finely grated lime peel
3 large eggs
5 large egg yolks
2 cups whipping cream
1½ cups whole milk
2½ teaspoons vanilla extract
¼ teaspoon salt

Lime slices (optional)

Preheat oven to 325°F. Place eight ⅔-cup ramekins or custard cups on work surface. Stir 1⅓ cups sugar and ½ cup water in heavy medium saucepan over low heat until sugar dissolves. Increase heat; boil without stirring until syrup turns deep amber, brushing down sides of pan with wet pastry brush and swirling pan occasionally, about 8 minutes. Immediately pour caramel into ramekins. Using oven mitts as aid, pick up each ramekin and tilt and rotate to coat sides with caramel. Place ramekins in large roasting pan.

Using back of spoon, mash ½ cup sugar and lime peel in large bowl until sugar is moist and fragrant. Add eggs and yolks; whisk to blend. Bring cream and milk to boil in heavy medium saucepan. Gradually whisk cream mixture into egg mixture. Whisk in vanilla and salt. Ladle custard into caramel-lined ramekins. Pour enough hot water into roasting pan to come halfway up sides of ramekins. Bake flans until just set and beginning to color on top, about 45 minutes. Remove from water; let cool 45 minutes. Cover and refrigerate flans overnight.

Cut around sides of ramekins to loosen flans. Invert flans onto plates. Garnish with lime slices, if desired.

8 SERVINGS

IN HOT WATER

While you may not be familiar with the word *bain-marie*, it's likely you know and use the technique. Bain-marie is the French term for a combination of cooking pans that gently cook delicate foods in water. In English it's called a water bath.

A bain-marie consists of a large pan, usually a roasting pan, in which a smaller pan (or pans) containing food is placed. The larger pan is filled with hot water, usually to a level that is about halfway up the sides of the smaller container. The entire contraption is put into the oven. The water heats up (but should not be allowed to boil) and gently cooks the food, typically something that incorporates eggs and/or cream, such as custards or puddings (the flans at left make use of this technique). These require gentle and consistent heat in order to prevent curdling.

Placing the bain-marie in the oven without spilling the water can be tricky. A tip from the *Bon Appétit* test kitchen: Before adding the water, open the oven door and pull out the rack halfway. Place the roasting pan (containing the smaller pan) on the rack, and use a teakettle to pour hot water into the roasting pan. Then slide the rack and pan into the oven.

❖ ❖ ❖

◆ FROZEN DESSERTS ◆

Chocolate Mint Sundaes

◆ ◆ ◆

1	cup water
1	cup sugar
½	cup thinly sliced fresh mint leaves
⅔	cup unsweetened cocoa powder (preferably Dutch-process)
4	tablespoons (½ stick) unsalted butter, room temperature

Mint chocolate chip ice cream
Fresh mint sprigs

Stir 1 cup water and sugar in heavy small saucepan over medium heat until sugar dissolves; bring syrup to boil. Remove from heat. Stir in mint leaves. Let stand 1 hour. Using slotted spoon, remove mint leaves from syrup. Whisk cocoa into syrup. Bring to boil. Add butter and whisk until smooth. Refrigerate sauce uncovered until cold. *(Can be made 1 week ahead. Cover and keep refrigerated.)*

Place 2 scoops of ice cream in each of 6 bowls. Drizzle each sundae with sauce; garnish with mint sprigs.

6 SERVINGS

Here's a remarkably easy, yet elegantly flavored dessert (opposite) to have on a hot summer's night. Make the mint-scented chocolate sauce up to a week ahead of time.

◆ ◆ ◆

Banana Ice Cream

◆ ◆ ◆

4	ripe bananas, peeled, mashed
1	14-ounce can sweetened condensed milk
¾	cup whipping cream

Combine bananas and condensed milk in large bowl. Whisk in cream. Pour banana mixture into 8 x 8 x 2-inch glass baking dish. Cover and freeze until softly set, stirring occasionally, about 2 hours. Transfer to large bowl. Using electric mixer, beat ice cream just until fluffy. Return to same glass dish. Cover and freeze until firm, about 6 hours. *(Can be made 3 days ahead. Keep frozen.)*

6 SERVINGS

Fresh Ginger and Citrus Sorbet

◆ ◆ ◆

Lemon and lime team up with fresh ginger in this cooling sorbet. It's a great ending for a light meal, since it's low in calories and has almost no fat and no cholesterol at all.

◆ ◆ ◆

5   cups water
2   cups sugar
3   tablespoons finely chopped peeled fresh ginger

2   teaspoons finely grated lemon peel
2   teaspoons finely grated lime peel
3   tablespoons fresh lemon juice
3   tablespoons fresh lime juice

   Fresh mint sprigs

Combine 5 cups water, sugar and ginger in heavy large saucepan. Bring to boil, stirring until sugar dissolves. Reduce heat and simmer 10 minutes. Strain into large bowl; discard solids.

Return liquid to same saucepan. Add lemon and lime peels. Boil 2 minutes. Remove from heat. Whisk in lemon and lime juices. Cool completely. Pour mixture into 13 x 9 x 2-inch glass baking dish. Cover and freeze until solid, about 6 hours or overnight.

Transfer mixture to processor and puree until smooth. Return to same glass dish; cover and freeze until solid, at least 3 hours or overnight. *(Can be prepared 3 days ahead. Keep frozen.)* Scoop sorbet into glasses or bowls. Garnish with mint.

8 SERVINGS

Strawberry Sundaes with Crème Fraîche Ice Cream

◆ ◆ ◆

1   cup half and half
1   cup whipping cream
½   vanilla bean, split lengthwise

¾   cup sugar
6   large egg yolks
1   cup crème fraîche*

1   1-pint basket strawberries, hulled, sliced
      Fresh Strawberry Sauce (see recipe opposite)

Combine half and half and cream in heavy large saucepan. Scrape in seeds from vanilla bean; add bean. Bring to boil. Remove from heat. Cover and let stand 15 minutes.

Using electric mixer, beat sugar and yolks in large bowl until thick and pale yellow, about 4 minutes. Gradually beat in warm cream mixture. Return mixture to saucepan. Stir over medium-low heat until custard thickens and leaves path on spoon when finger is drawn across, about 6 minutes (do not boil). Remove from heat. Cool 15 minutes. Discard vanilla bean. Whisk in crème fraîche. Cover and chill custard until cold, about 3 hours.

Process custard in ice cream maker according to manufacturer's instructions. Transfer ice cream to covered container. Freeze until firm. *(Can be made 3 days ahead. Keep frozen.)*

Place 2 scoops of crème fraîche ice cream in each of 6 bowls. Top with sliced strawberries and strawberry sauce.

*Available at some supermarkets. If unavailable, heat 1 cup whipping cream to lukewarm (85°F). Remove from heat and mix in 2 tablespoons buttermilk. Cover and let stand in warm draft-free area until slightly thickened, 24 to 48 hours, depending on temperature of room. Refrigerate until ready to use.

6 SERVINGS

The French specialty of thickened cream, called crème fraîche, is what gives this exceptional ice cream irresistible tang and a silky texture. A simple fresh strawberry sauce is all that's needed to top it.

◆ ◆ ◆

Fresh Strawberry Sauce

1   16-ounce basket strawberries, hulled, coarsely chopped
½   cup sugar
1   teaspoon fresh lemon juice

Stir berries, sugar and juice in heavy medium saucepan over medium heat until sugar dissolves. Bring to boil. Reduce heat and simmer 3 minutes. Transfer sauce to bowl. Chill until cold, 2 hours. *(Can be made 1 day ahead. Cover; keep chilled.)*

MAKES ABOUT 2 CUPS

The graham cracker crunch topping is delicious on its own, but combined with ripe peaches, cinnamon syrup and ice cream, it makes for positively addictive sundaes.

◆ ◆ ◆

Cinnamon-Crunch Peach Sundaes

◆ ◆ ◆

1	cup plus 6½ tablespoons sugar
¾	cup water
6	tablespoons dark corn syrup
3	cinnamon sticks, broken in half
6	whole cinnamon graham crackers, crushed to coarse crumbs
4½	tablespoons unsalted butter, melted
6	medium peaches, pitted, sliced into wedges
1½	tablespoons fresh lemon juice
¾	teaspoon ground cinnamon
	French vanilla ice cream
6	cinnamon sticks (optional)

Stir 1 cup plus 2 tablespoons sugar, ¾ cup water, corn syrup and halved cinnamon sticks in heavy medium saucepan over medium heat until sugar dissolves; bring to boil. Reduce heat to low;

simmer until reduced to 1½ cups, about 20 minutes. Cool; remove cinnamon sticks. *(Can be made 1 week ahead. Cover; chill.)*

Preheat oven to 350°F. Combine cracker crumbs, butter and 1½ tablespoons sugar in small bowl; toss to coat evenly. Spread mixture out on small baking sheet. Bake until golden, stirring occasionally, about 5 minutes. Cool topping.

Mix sliced peaches, 3 tablespoons sugar, lemon juice and ground cinnamon in medium bowl. Let stand until juices form, at least 15 minutes and up to 1 hour.

Place 2 scoops of ice cream in each of 6 bowls. Spoon peaches and juices over ice cream. Drizzle with syrup and sprinkle with crunch topping. Garnish with cinnamon sticks, if desired.

6 SERVINGS

Raspberry Hot Fudge Sundaes

◆ ◆ ◆

¾	cup sugar
½	cup half and half
4	ounces unsweetened chocolate, chopped
2	tablespoons light corn syrup
1	tablespoon unsalted butter
⅛	teaspoon salt
2	tablespoons framboise eau-de-vie (clear raspberry brandy)

Vanilla ice cream
Fresh raspberries

Stir sugar, half and half, chocolate, corn syrup, butter and salt in heavy medium saucepan over low heat until sugar dissolves and chocolate melts. Increase heat to medium-low and cook until sauce is smooth and thick, stirring constantly, about 4 minutes. Remove sauce from heat. Stir in framboise. *(Can be made 1 week ahead. Cover and chill. Rewarm over low heat, stirring frequently.)*

For each serving, spoon 1 tablespoon sauce into sundae glass or wine goblet. Top with 2 scoops of ice cream. Spoon 3 tablespoons sauce over. Sprinkle raspberries over and serve immediately.

6 SERVINGS

ALL ABOUT LIQUEURS

Any distilled spirit that has been sweetened and flavored is a liqueur. But a term by which liqueurs are also known better describes the role they play in cooking and entertaining: *cordials*. Indeed, liqueurs promote a convivial air when served at the conclusion of a meal, as a topping for ice cream, or as a potent dessert flavoring.

While the spirits on which they are based vary from Cognac to rum, whiskey to neutral spirits, liqueurs are generally classified by their flavorings.

◆ Fruit Liqueurs: These include stone fruit, such as cherries, peaches and apricots; berries; tropical fruit; and citrus fruit, among which the most famous are orange liqueurs, generally classified as curaçaos.

◆ Herb Liqueurs: Among a wide variety, there are those based on time-honored, monastic blends of herbs, including French Bénédictine and Swiss Chartreuse; and those in which one herb, such as anise or mint, predominates.

◆ Bean and Nut Liqueurs: These feature the distinctive flavors of coffee, chocolate or nuts.

◆ Miscellaneous Liqueurs: These combine the above categories or add other novel twists, such as cream or eggs.

◆ ◆ ◆

KINDS OF COCONUT

Snowy-white coconut adds incredible richness and a hint of exotic flavor to many dishes, both sweet and savory. Depending on the type of recipe you're preparing and the effect you want, you can buy coconut in several different ready-to-use forms.

Shreds, flakes or finely ground particles of coconut contribute texture along with flavor to baked goods and desserts, as well as some savory dishes. You can find these products in cans or plastic bags in the baking section of most markets. Read the label carefully to see whether a particular item is sweetened or unsweetened. Keep them refrigerated after opening.

Coconut milk, which is available sweetened, unsweetened and in a "light" version, is a liquid extracted from the meat of the coconut, sold in cans or bottles in the bakery section of supermarkets. Cream of coconut, also extracted from the coconut meat, is usually found in the liquor department at the supermarket. As their names imply, coconut milk tends to be thinner and cream of coconut richer and thicker. Both add flavor and smoothness to soups, sauces, beverages and batters. Thick, sweetened versions can be used in desserts and drinks.

◆ ◆ ◆

◆ COOKIES ◆

Almond-scented Macaroons

◆ ◆ ◆

1½ cups (packed) shredded sweetened coconut (about 6 ounces)
6 tablespoons sweetened condensed milk
1 tablespoon all purpose flour
1 teaspoon vanilla extract
¼ teaspoon almond extract
Dash of salt

Preheat oven to 350°F. Butter 2 heavy large baking sheets. Combine all ingredients in large bowl; stir to blend well. Drop dough by scant tablespoonfuls onto prepared baking sheets, spacing 1½ inches apart. Shape cookies into small mounds, about 1 inch in diameter. Press tops slightly to flatten. Bake until pale golden, about 8 minutes. Transfer each baking sheet to rack. Cool cookies on sheets 5 minutes. Using metal spatula, transfer cookies to racks and cool completely. *(Can be prepared up to 3 days ahead. Store in airtight container at room temperature.)*

MAKES ABOUT 2 DOZEN

Pumpkin Bars

◆ ◆ ◆

2 cups all purpose flour
2 cups sugar
1 tablespoon ground cinnamon
2 teaspoons baking powder
1 teaspoon baking soda
1 teaspoon salt
½ teaspoon ground nutmeg
½ teaspoon ground cloves
1 15-ounce can solid pack pumpkin
4 large eggs
¾ cup vegetable oil
1 cup raisins

6   ounces cream cheese, room temperature

1   cup powdered sugar

⅓   cup butter, room temperature

Preheat oven to 350°F. Grease 15½ x 10½ x 1-inch baking sheet. Stir first 8 ingredients in large bowl to blend. Add pumpkin, eggs and oil and beat until blended. Mix in raisins. Spread batter in prepared pan. Bake until tester inserted into center comes out clean, about 25 minutes. Cool cake in pan on rack.

Beat cream cheese, powdered sugar and butter in medium bowl to blend. Spread frosting over cake in thin layer. *(Can be prepared 1 day ahead. Refrigerate until cold, then cover and keep refrigerated.)* Cut cake into bars and serve.

MAKES 24

Butter Cookies with Raisins

◆ ◆ ◆

¾   cup (1½ sticks) unsalted butter, room temperature

⅔   cup sugar

½   teaspoon salt

1½   teaspoons vanilla extract

1¾   cups all purpose flour

½   cup raisins

Using electric mixer, beat butter, sugar and salt in large bowl until creamy. Mix in vanilla. Add flour and raisins; mix until smooth dough forms. Divide dough in half. Shape each dough half into 1½-inch-diameter log. Wrap each log in plastic; refrigerate until firm, about 2 hours. *(Can be made 3 days ahead. Keep chilled.)*

Preheat oven to 375°F. Butter 2 large baking sheets. Cut each dough log into ¼-inch-thick slices. Place slices on prepared baking sheets, spacing 1 inch apart. Bake until cookies are golden, about 10 minutes. Cool slightly on baking sheets. Transfer to racks; cool completely. *(Can be made 3 days ahead. Store in airtight container at room temperature.)*

MAKES ABOUT 3 DOZEN

◆ ◆ ◆

These cake-like treats are made moist by the pumpkin and spicy by ground nutmeg and cloves. They're great paired with a tall glass of milk.

◆ ◆ ◆

Ten-Minute Microwave Brownies

◆ ◆ ◆

Nonstick vegetable oil spray
2 large eggs
¼ cup (½ stick) unsalted butter, melted, cooled
1 teaspoon vanilla extract
1 cup sugar
½ cup unsweetened cocoa powder
½ cup all purpose flour
⅓ cup semisweet or white chocolate chips
⅓ cup coarsely chopped macadamia nuts

Spray 8 x 8 x 2-inch glass baking dish with nonstick spray. Whisk eggs, butter and vanilla in large bowl to blend. Add sugar, cocoa and flour and blend well. Stir in chocolate chips and nuts. Spread batter in prepared dish.

Cook brownies uncovered in microwave on high until tester inserted into center comes out clean, about 5 minutes. Cool 5 minutes; cut into squares. Serve warm or at room temperature.

MAKES 16

◆ ◆ ◆

No joke: These amazing treats take only about ten minutes to make, start to finish. They're even better with mint chocolate chip ice cream.

◆ ◆ ◆

Lime Bars with Coconut Crust

◆ ◆ ◆

CRUST
2¼ cups sweetened flaked coconut (about 6½ ounces)
¾ cup finely ground sugar cookies (about 3½ ounces)
3 tablespoons unsalted butter, melted

LIME CURD
¾ cup sugar
½ cup fresh lime juice
¼ cup (½ stick) unsalted butter
1½ tablespoons yellow cornmeal
1 teaspoon grated lime peel
Pinch of salt
4 large egg yolks

Powdered sugar

FOR CRUST: Preheat oven to 325°F. Mix coconut, cookies and butter in large bowl to blend. Transfer 2 cups coconut mixture to

8 x 8 x 2-inch baking pan. Press over bottom and ¾ inch up sides of pan. Reserve remaining coconut mixture for topping. Bake crust until light golden, about 15 minutes.

FOR LIME CURD: Combine first 6 ingredients in large metal bowl. Set bowl over saucepan of simmering water (do not allow bottom of bowl to touch water). Whisk until sugar dissolves and cornmeal is tender, about 10 minutes. Add egg yolks and whisk until lime curd mixture thickens, about 7 minutes.

Pour lime curd into crust. Sprinkle reserved coconut mixture over curd. Bake until curd is set and topping is golden brown, about 10 minutes. Transfer pan to rack. Cool completely. *(Can be prepared 8 hours ahead. Cover and store at room temperature.)*

Cut into bars. Sprinkle with powdered sugar and serve.

6 SERVINGS

Langues-de-Chat

◆ ◆ ◆

¼   cup (½ stick) unsalted butter, room temperature
¼   cup sugar
½   teaspoon grated lemon peel
½   teaspoon vanilla extract
¼   cup egg whites (about 2 large)
6   tablespoons all purpose flour
    Pinch of salt

Preheat oven to 350°F. Butter 2 large baking sheets. Using electric mixer, beat butter and sugar in medium bowl until well blended. Beat in lemon peel and vanilla. Add egg whites and beat 30 seconds. Add flour and salt; beat just until blended.

Spoon batter into pastry bag fitted with ⅓-inch plain round tip. Pipe batter onto baking sheets in 2½-inch-long strips, spacing 2 inches apart. Bake until edges are golden, about 10 minutes. Transfer cookies to racks; cool (cookies will crisp as they cool). *(Can be made 2 days ahead. Store airtight at room temperature.)*

MAKES ABOUT 2½ DOZEN

◆ ◆ ◆

The name, literally translated as "cats' tongues," refers to the shape of these delicate, crisp cookies. They can be made up to two days ahead.

◆ ◆ ◆

Here's a real treat for the lunch box. Adding dried cherries and chocolate chips turns these classic cookies into something new. Have them with the Raspberry Hot Fudge Sundaes (right) from page 213.

◆ ◆ ◆

Cherry-Chocolate Chip Oatmeal Cookies

◆ ◆ ◆

1   cup all purpose flour
½   teaspoon baking soda
¼   teaspoon salt
½   cup plus 2 tablespoons (1¼ sticks) unsalted butter, room temperature
½   cup sugar
½   cup (packed) dark brown sugar
1   large egg
1   teaspoon vanilla extract
½   teaspoon almond extract
1   cup old-fashioned oats
1½   cups semisweet chocolate chips
1   cup dried tart cherries
½   cup slivered almonds, toasted

Position racks in center and top third of oven and preheat to 325°F. Line 2 large baking sheets with parchment paper. Sift flour, baking soda and salt into medium bowl. Using electric mixer, beat butter, sugar and brown sugar in large bowl until well blended. Mix in egg and both extracts. Beat in flour mixture. Mix in oats, then chocolate chips, cherries and almonds.

Drop dough by rounded tablespoonfuls onto baking sheets, spacing 2 inches apart. Bake cookies 12 minutes. Switch and rotate baking sheets. Bake cookies until golden, about 6 minutes longer. Cool cookies on sheets (cookies will firm as they cool). *(Can be prepared 1 week ahead. Store airtight at room temperature.)*

MAKES ABOUT 2 DOZEN

Spicy Sugar Cookies

◆ ◆ ◆

2   cups all purpose flour
2   teaspoons fine sea salt or salt
1   teaspoon black pepper
¼   teaspoon cayenne pepper
¾   cup (1½ sticks) unsalted butter, room temperature
½   cup sugar
1   large egg
1   teaspoon vanilla extract
1   teaspoon finely minced peeled fresh ginger

Mix flour, salt, black pepper and cayenne pepper in medium bowl. Using electric mixer, beat butter and sugar in large bowl until well blended. Beat in egg, vanilla extract and ginger. Add dry ingredients and beat just until blended. Form dough into ball. Wrap in plastic; refrigerate at least 2 hours and up to 1 day.

Preheat oven to 350°F. Divide dough into 3 equal pieces. Roll each piece of dough between palms of hands and floured work surface to form 1¼-inch-diameter log. Cut logs into ¼-inch-thick slices. Place on ungreased baking sheets.

Bake cookies until set but still very pale, about 12 minutes. Cool cookies on racks. *(Can be made 2 days ahead. Store cookies in airtight container at room temperature.)*

MAKES ABOUT 5 DOZEN

SAVORING SALT

Any cooking teacher worth his or her salt will tell you that this humble seasoning is a culinary hero. Salt preserves meat and fish by drawing out moisture. It also serves as a meat tenderizer and helps develop the flavor of wheat in breads. But not all salt is the same. Here are four different kinds.

◆ Table Salt: Mechanically removed from rock-salt deposits, this common salt form is used in virtually all recipes—even desserts.

◆ Kosher Salt: Originally used to draw blood from meat to comply with Jewish dietary laws, kosher salt works very well in brines for pickling fresh vegetables and other foods because it contains no additives or trace metals.

◆ Sea Salt: This kind of salt, harvested from the Mediterranean Sea, contains only pure sodium chloride, nothing more. The resulting crystals, whether coarse or fine, all have a fairly standardized flavor.

◆ Fleur de Sel: These fragrant "flower of salt" bright-white crystals are actually the top layer of sea salt from the marshlands of Brittany.

◆ ◆ ◆

·I{\footnotesize NDEX}·

Page numbers in *italics* indicate color photographs.

Acknowledgments

◆ ◆ ◆

The following people contributed the recipes included in this book: Tom Aikens, Pied-à-Terre, London, England; Anse Chastenet, St. Lucia, British West Indies; John Ash; Mary Barber; Melanie Barnard; Paul Bertolli; Lena Cederham Birnbaum; Carole Bloom; Leslie Beal Bloom; Flo Braker; Frank Brigtsen, Brigtsen's, New Orleans, Louisiana; Stephen Bull, Stephen Bull St. Martin's Lane, London, England; Campton Place Restaurant, San Francisco, California; Sally Clarke, Clarke's, London, England; Cockney's Pie and Mash, London, England; Commander's Palace, New Orleans, Louisiana; Sara Corpening; Cranks, London, England; Myrna Crawford; Eric Crouillere-Chavot, Chavot, London, England; Lane Crowther; The Culinary Institute of America, Hyde Park, New York; Jane Cunningham; Brooke Dojny; Jodi and Jeff DuFresne; Eli's, Block Island, Rhode Island; Elizabeth Ellis; Merle Ellis; Sue Reddin Ellison; Tarla Fallgatter; Susan Feniger, Border Grill, Santa Monica, California; Barbara Pool Fenzl; Janet Fletcher; Jim Fobel; Fourways Inn, Paget, Bermuda; The Franklin, London, England; The Garden, Philadelphia, Pennsylvania; Laureen Gauthier; Paul Gayler, The Lanesborough Conservatory, London, England; George Germon, Al Forno, Providence, Rhode Island; Sarah Griffiths; Sophie Grigson; Lauren Groveman; Kathy Gunst; Ken Haedrich; Fergus Henderson, St. John, London, England; Bruce Horton; Hotel Santa Caterina, Amalfi, Italy; Philip Howard, The Square, London, England; Seemi Iqbal; Johnson & Wales University, Providence, Rhode Island; Michele Anna Jordan; Karen Kaplan; Renée Kasman, Zola, Nashville, Tennessee; Mollie Katzen; Jeanne Thiel Kelley; Martin Kelley; Kristine Kidd; Johanne Killeen, Al Forno, Providence, Rhode Island; Elinor Klivans; Gary Krolikowski; La Bastide de Moustiers, La Grisolière, Moustiers-Sainte-Marie, France; Le Cordon Bleu, Paris, France; Ron Lento; Magnolia Grill, Durham, North Carolina; Michael McLaughlin; Mary Sue Milliken, Border Grill, Santa Monica, California; Jinx and Jefferson Morgan; Selma Brown Morrow; Jean-Christophe Novelli, Les Saveurs de Jean-Christophe Novelli, London, England; James O'Shea; Rochelle Palermo; Debra Paquette, Zola, Nashville, Tennessee; Diane Parr; Eve Plimmer; Thane Prince; Gordon Ramsay, Aubergine, London, England; Gary Rhodes, City Rhodes, London, England; Mary Risley; River's End Restaurant, Jenner, California; Louise and Dave Robinson; Rick Rodgers; Betty Rosbottom; Patti and Al Shapiro; Sharon Shuford; Marie Simmons; Joseph Simone, Tosca, Hingham, Massachusetts; Sally Anne Smith; Renie Steves; John Taylor; Sarah Tenaglia; Mary Jo Thoresen; Alina Tugend; Szeto Tze-Bun, Grand Hyatt, Hong Kong; Valentino, Los Angeles, California; Jennifer Viegas; Gianni Vietina; Marcus Wareing, L'Oranger, London, England; Joanne Weir; Anne Willan; Matt Yohalem, Bistro 315, Santa Fe, New Mexico.

The following people contributed the photographs included in this book: Noel Barnhurst; David Bishop; Walter P. Calahan; Wendy Carlson; Steve Cohen; Wyatt Counts; Julie Dennis; Owen Franken; Beth Galton; Greg Gillis; Michael Goldman; Laura Johansen; John Kane; John Kelly; Deborah Klesenski; Michael La Riche; Brian Leatart; Paul Moore; Gary Moss; Maria Robledo; David Roth; Jeff Sarpa; Shaffer-Smith; Ellen Silverman; Spathis & Miller; Rick Szczechowski; Mark Thomas; Elizabeth Watt.

Front jacket photo: Mark Thomas, Photographer; Dora Johenson, Food Stylist; Nancy Micklin, Prop Stylist.